The Baby and the Beast

By

Brad Martin

DEDICATION

This first thank you might shock some people as you delve into this book, but I would like to dedicate this book to my brother, without whom I would not have developed into the warm compassionate human being I am today. I would also like to dedicate this book to those people who, and you know who you are, have helped me through the years. There have been many ways people have helped me, but the BEST way they have helped me is by believing in me.

PROLOGUE

Let me start first by saying that this is in NO PART the WHOLE story of my life. For the whole story of my life I would have to ask my parents certain things, and I do NOT want them to know that I have written this book. Of course, if it helps as many people as I want it to help, then they are definitely going to know what I have done, and only then will I be FORCED to tell them. I will of course be using different names for the members of my family in this book, if I even use names for them at all. I will NOT, however, be using a different name for myself because, after all, this is my book and how are you supposed to know I wrote it if I don't tell you who I am? If my brother was ever to find out I had written this book, it would most assuredly mean my death. If my mother was to find out I had written this book, she would most assuredly be driven to a mental institution for life, or worse... of course, all this is just speculation on my part, but I am not willing to find out if my speculations will turn into the truth...

This book is, first and foremost about helping and healing people. I'm not writing this book to make myself a famous author. I'm not writing this book to get tons of money so I can stick it to my former bosses, although that would be a fun idea. I'm writing this book for one reason and one reason only. I'm writing this book to buy that million-dollar house I've always dreamed of, I'm just kidding. The REAL reason I'm writing this book is so that maybe one person, although I hope it's more, will be helped by it. My hope is that by writing this book I can get people talking and discussing aspects of their lives so that others know what's going on in them. My hope is that by reading this book, and possibly having discussions about this book, people can begin to open up about their lives and share what's unique about themselves, share what's been bothering them, or share what they've been going through in their lives, both in the present and in the past. My REAL hope for this book is...UNITY.

PREFACE

This is an advisory to anyone reading this book. Although I don't think this book needs an advisory because of the freedom of speech amendment, I am warning anyone who reads this book that parts of it are going to be a little bit sexually graphic. I make this warning not out of a sense of shock value, but out of a sense of morality for any minor or any adult who lets a minor read this book. I do, however, hope that if you don't let your child read this book because of its graphic nature that you do at least read it yourself. Maybe you can come away with questions to ask your children, or even answers to your children's questions.

TABLE OF CONTENTS

CHAPTER 1:
WHERE IT ALL BEGINS

I was born April 21, 1975 and I know almost nothing about the first five years of my life, but throughout the ENTIRE decade of the 1980's and the first half of the 1990's I was told straight to my face that I was worthless. Just those words, 'you're worthless', can do a whole lot of damage to a young impressionable mind which hasn't yet been molded. My parents praised me a lot, but I didn't hear those words at all, I heard the negative words of the people who weren't even related to me because, to me, those words were the truth. Parents have to say that they love you and that you're a good kid, regardless of what they really think, because they are your parents and they are supposed to set a good example and praise their children...right? The words, 'you're worthless', have stayed with me until this very day, and I think about them all the time.

Let me introduce you to the principal characters in my life, there are five. Although there will be many bit part players and many who will have changed my life dramatically, these five principal participants are the ones that have my last name. If you'll notice, I didn't call them family...the reason for that is because one of them never acted, to me, like they embodied the word 'FAMILY'. The word FAMILY, to me, means a person, or persons, who would do anything for another person within the same family, if not illegal or immoral, regardless of the return that they would get out of it. Let's start with the oldest first.

My dad was a military man, UNITED STATES AIR FORCE. I

1

don't know exactly what he did; heck, to a little kid like me he was just the guy who brought home the money. My dad taught me valuable lessons on many occasions, but on one day in particular he taught me a lesson that I will never forget. My dad taught me this lesson not by speaking, but by walking away.

One day we were at a bowling alley, doing what else but bowling, and we were in the parking lot getting ready to get in the car. Apparently he'd had some words inside with a guy because this big guy came up from behind and started talking to my dad in a raised voice. This happened for reasons I didn't understand because I wasn't privy to any altercation, if there was one, before this one. I don't know exactly what they were saying, but I could see that things were getting very heated. I was no more than eleven or twelve at the time and what was going through my mind was that my dad was going to get his ass kicked. I mean, he was in the military, but he was NO tough guy with a six-pack who could beat up anyone who he had a problem with. . The guy was still saying things to my dad in a heated voice and my dad (my hero) just turned around and walked away…and that's the last thing I remember.

I thought to myself right then and there that I wanted to be just like my father…he's an inspiration to me for a lot of things, but mostly he's an inspiration to me for just having the courage to walk away.

My dad also is the embodiment to me of what a caring family man should be like. He has a wife he dotes on hand and foot, three kids that he would basically do ANYTHING for, and you just don't see that in a lot of families, or at least I don't anyway. He is the kind of person that if you spill something on the counter, he has already got it cleaned up and dried off before you have a chance to grab a napkin...he is love.

That kind of love may be detrimental to some however. I believe it was detrimental to me a little bit just because of the fact that I am now thirty-two years of age and I still don't know how to do a lot of things for myself. In all fairness my father IS a great man and although I would change a lot of things, I would not change him one bit, my father is the most loving, caring person I know.

I think my mother had the hardest occupation in this world. My mother was a stay-at-home mom. I bet you're thinking to yourself right now, "Yeah right, stay-at-home mom, you mean she didn't want to actually have to go out of the house and, God forbid, actually EARN a living instead of sitting on the sofa all day watching soap operas". Some mothers get bad raps because of being stay-at-home moms. To the non-stay-at-home moms I challenge them to do what the stay-at-home moms do for maybe one week and see for themselves that it's no easy task. NO, she didn't have that nine-to-five job while the kids were at school, but she was where she was needed back then.

My mother was at home to take phone calls from kids' teachers when the kids got in trouble. My mom was the kids' chauffeur to anywhere they happened to need to go. I can remember my mom taking me to middle school on several occasions when we lived in England, she didn't have to because I took a bus, but that's the kind of person she was. My mother would do anything for her family.

Now my mom is a stay-at-home mom when she doesn't need to be. Illness has taken all the pep out of her. She has depression and other problems where there used to be life. She's on a steady regimen of pills morning, noon and night. I wouldn't wish the life she has right now on anyone because it looks to me like a very painful and confusing way to live. I am, however, blessed that she is on this planet because without her the world wouldn't have gained me.

That brings me to one of the most influential principal characters in my life, my sister. I don't know all that much about her to tell you the truth. I'm at least three years younger than her so that meant we ran in different social circles. I will never forget though how whenever I would have a nightmare, as kids often do…the boogeyman and such, I would always go across the hall into her room and I would always be welcome to slip under the covers with her…I love her for her kindness, warmth, and sensitivity. She was a person I could confide in totally when I couldn't tell my parents anything. She would oftentimes listen to me and give me advice on what to do...she was, and still continues to be, great.

Then of course she got involved with a man that used to be her husband and at that point in time I felt I couldn't tell her anything because her attitude was just so totally different. Even though she was going through her own torment at the time, she never really lost sight of the big picture. She was always there for me when I needed her, she had a great sense of humor and I wouldn't trade her for anything in the world...I love my sister. The only good thing to come out of that marriage, in my mind, was my niece.

After she got away from this man she joined the military, or maybe she joined the military shortly before…I forget that stuff sometimes…anyhow she got stationed in Japan. While in Japan she got married again and had another child. She has a total of four girls now, all living angels to me, and a husband that treats her well and with respect and dignity. Truth be told I really wish my sister hadn't gone off to Japan. She was being stationed in Japan for personal reasons, but when she left I felt I'd lost my best friend.

Now we move on to the central character in this whole book, my brother. He was a typical kid who played and had fun. There were days when we would actually team up and kind of torment my sister...ahh to be young again. Something happened to him and he changed. I'm not sure where he skewed away from the person he was because I didn't really notice or recognize the signs that he had changed, but I knew he had made a drastic ninety degree change and he would never be the same person he was. I think the seeds for his change were planted in Omaha because that's when he decided to run away; but that will be discussed later on in this book. I don't really know for sure...all I know is that the brother I knew for a very short time had been lost forever and a new sinister, more devious one put in his place.

I think most of all my brother became a victim of peer pressure, and now he is ruled by drink. He casually mentions to me that he drinks every night, and once or twice he has told me about his pot usage. I don't know if that's his way of trying to cry for help or that he is somehow proud of the fact that he drinks and smokes pot. Don't get me wrong, I'm not trying to vilify my brother, I'm just explaining what he did. I have no clue why he did what he did and I know for a fact that he is going through his own torment, and that he has to live with his own demons.

My dad and mom had moved around a lot by the time I came into this world, and when I did come into it they were still moving around so I got indoctrinated into the life of a military family.

My mom tells me I was conceived in Greece. My mom also tells me that there was some kind of tiff or war or something going on there so they got out quick, otherwise that's where I would have been born. I was actually not born in Greece; I was born in Omaha, Nebraska. My sister, who is the oldest, also has the distinction of being born in Omaha, Nebraska as well. With being a military family and being moved around a lot I think it is SO cool that we were born not only in the same country and not even only in the same state, but in the SAME hospital. My brother, who was born second, was born in California, I don't remember what city, and frankly I don't care. If it seems like that statement has a lot of animosity in it...IT DOES. You'll see later on in this book why I've grown to dislike him so much, but I'm getting ahead of myself.

It was a miracle that I survived my birth because when I was born I didn't want to breathe and I didn't want to eat. This is gleaned from things that I have heard because as I said, I will NEVER ask my parents for information as I don't want them to know about this book. I was diagnosed as spastic quadriplegic and I wasn't ever supposed to walk. I saw somebody a few years back who was diagnosed with virtually the same thing and his life took a much more dramatic turn...death at a very early age. I didn't know this at that time, but when my mother was pregnant with me she was taking Valium...all the way up until about the third month. She still blames herself for having done that, but I don't blame her one bit now because I have all that I need from her...LOVE. I am just so blessed to be alive because she could have been one of those mothers that say to hell with it and keep doing what they're doing regardless of the consequences to baby. She stopped taking the Valium, I think it was for depression based on what I know now, and she went ahead and had that baby, and that baby has no regrets or questions whatsoever about any of it. He is just so happy to be alive and to be able to experience all of life's ups and downs and get to play the game...and maybe even win big someday; thank you MOM and DAD for having me.

I was told some things later on in my life that lead me to believe I was either one very disturbed or just one very goofy child. I was told by my mother that one day when I was really small I was sitting in my highchair eating some food with a plastic spoon. She turned away for some reason and when she turned back around I had taken the spoon, dug it right into my eye and now had a nice little slice down my eye. I am also told by my mother that when I was younger I was walking around the living room and I lost my balance, going headfirst into a vase. There have been a couple of comments over the years about my header into the vase like, "Was that the Greek vase I remember that you bought when you were stationed there?" And, "I think I remember that came in a set, right?"

I also hear a story about when I had some surgery done, I don't remember if the surgery was done on my forehead or my eye. I had the operation and I was AWAKE for the whole procedure, and what's more amazing is that I was asking them questions...I'm glad I don't remember the questions. When I was done in surgery we went to the commissary, or the supermarket for those of you not in the military...I guess it wasn't one of those stay overnight surgeries. We went into the commissary and I was put in the front seat of the shopping cart, as most young children are, and I told my parents, "I want... to... tell... you... something... zzzzz." And I kept repeating this over and over again going down each of the aisles; my mom says she never did figure out what I was trying to tell her.

There is also another time when it was my sister's turn to tell a story about me, a short one anyway. My sister said that when I was younger I bit the foot right off of her Barbie doll. Apparently I was old enough to get an allowance because she said that as punishment for doing it she made me go down to the store and buy her another one just like it.

I've gone through many diagnoses in my life, the latest one which is hard to pronounce is pontoneocerrebellurhypoplasia. I have no clue what that means at all, but when I was born I was diagnosed with congenital 5th nerve anesthesia, which basically means from the lower part of my eyes all the way to the top of my head I can't feel a thing. Congenital 5th nerve anesthesia affects reflexes, and the sensation of that nerve. I was always bumping into things because I also have motor function problems, which also has to do with the 5th nerve. I had to wear a helmet for some of my young life. As a result of all these bumps and bruises to my head, I had a bunch of scar tissue right in the middle of my forehead. I don't remember whether it formed after many falls or if they put it in there to protect my head…I don't really care, all I know is that I felt like the elephant man. I had to go to school with this helmet on my head and I felt so out of place that I felt like an outcast. It wasn't a normal looking helmet, like for example a jet-black helmet like all the motorcyclists were wearing; that would have been so cool. I would have been so proud to wear that kind of helmet and it probably would have given me more confidence too as I was a very timid little boy.

My helmet was a HUGE white helmet with quarter-sized holes all over it, I guess to help my head breathe or something. I remember feeling so dorky in that helmet that most days I just wanted to crawl into a little hole and stay there until the problem with my forehead or my balance went away…it never did go away.

The thing that made wearing my helmet worse wasn't the fact that kids would tease me unmercifully about it, I came home in silent tears so my parents wouldn't know, it was the fact that my family and other people felt that they could decorate the helmet. There I was, this little boy in this WAY oversized white helmet with holes in it that was getting stickers put all over it. I remember very vividly that there were rainbow stickers on it as well...I was a damn sideshow freak basically instead of a normal little boy who just wanted to be loved and not ridiculed for what he looked like. To add to the misery, since I had an eyesight problem back then, I still do to this very day, I had to sit in the very front of the class where all the other kids could see me. All the kids could see my pitiful self with that huge oversized helmet on top of my head...those were not pleasant years in my life.

I've been through many surgeries in my young lifetime. When we were trying to get me SSI we had to itemize these visits and it came to well over two thousand hospital stays and appointments...I was barely twenty at the time. I've gone through a lot of forehead surgeries because of an imbalance in the brain that has caused me to fall down and break my head open several times. This caused scar tissue to form and became the start of relentless teasing at the hands of other children. I've also had many eye surgeries, resulting in a perforated cornea which has caused me to have 20/400 eyesight in one eye, the other one was about to perforate as well so they sewed it shut to save what they could; that eye is 20/80 on a good day now.

There was one particular time when an Army doctor decided he was going to help save the eye that I had. He did surgery on it, and then he put a big heavy patch of gauze on it and taped it up. Having the congenital 5th nerve anesthesia that I have I was unable to know what my eye was doing under that patch and I was unable to close it. Since I was unable to close that eye because of patch, the gauze was constantly rubbing against the eye and it caused me to be worse off than I already was. But on the upside my mom told me that even with my good eye patched up I was basically running laps all around that hospital.

That is unfortunately the extent of my knowledge about myself when I was younger. I would definitely add more if I could, and if I were brave enough to ask my parents or anybody else about my situation. However, they would then find out that I was writing this, and as I stated before things would not go well. Therefore, my parents and I are just much better off if I do not ask. I'm sorry if that makes for a more boring book than what it would have been, but suffice to say, if you want the Reader's Digest version, I went through a hell of a lot of surgeries and a diagnosis that I have far surpassed. I went through relentless teasing and I still came out of it with laughter, and humility…and this was all before my age even hit double digits.

CHAPTER 2:

MEETING THE DEVIL, THE FIRST TIME

This chapter is a little sexually charged when discussing certain people, you will find out in Chapter 3 why that is so.

My life started of course when I was born, but for the sake of the story of this part of my life we will start in Germany. I was very young then, about nine. I remember having so much fun there. I met my T-ball coach in Germany. I remember loving to go to T-ball all the time and how it made me feel so free; I also loved being part of a team…it made me feel wanted. Yes, it wasn't baseball, but with my eye problems my parents just couldn't see me trying to hit a ball that was flying straight at me. My parents probably said, "Let's find a sport where he can hit something stationary so at least he has a chance."

My T-ball coach was married and had a son when I first met him. I remember getting to spend the night at this guy's house. My sister and I were staying there together. MY coach's HOUSE, how cool was that? Too bad my sister had to come along. I have forgotten, and I don't care, where my brother was staying; there goes that darned animosity towards him again…you'll see why. I remember getting the privilege of playing on my coach's computer. We had certain times of the day that we could play on it, and I liked playing *Ghostbusters*, you know the popular movie, on his computer…that was a fun game. How I wish I had that time back again because I was so innocent and naive back then and had no forethought of what was going to happen next, I was just a kid enjoying the moment.

I went on the computer at a time when 'the grownups' said I wasn't supposed to, typical kid living for the moment and not afraid of the consequences but just enjoying the thrill of it all, so I lost my computer privileges for the duration of my stay at their house. I was SO bummed out about that I was pretty much sulking about it the rest of the day, but as kids do I rebounded quickly.

I remember it was around Christmas time because there was a BIG tree in the front room. Now that I think about it, that was the year my parents went to Omaha because my grandpa had died.

I can recall the day we first went into Omaha. I remember it like it was yesterday because I walked into the living room and saw both my grandparents there, and then I turned and saw my cousin Brandon lying there all sprawled out on the couch sort of like saying, 'This is my place and nobody better come disturb it.' Brandon was watching what would later become one of my most favorite movies: Superman 2. It became one of my favorite movies precisely because it reminds me of Brandon.

I walked over to the couch where he was sitting and he let me sit down and watch it with him. I had never seen him before and didn't know right off the bat who he was. I kind of regard it as his house basically because he was living in it, whereas I had just arrived there and we weren't going to stay long. The fact that he let me sit down on that couch and watch a movie with him, and that he interacted with me, was just such a great feeling to me that whenever I sit down and watch Superman 2, I ALWAYS think of my cousin Brandon and how much I loved him at that moment for inviting me into his realm so to speak. Brandon would also do other things with me. For instance, my grandpa had a huge basement and a dartboard down there and we would go down and play darts sometimes, as well as other silly kids' games.

When my brother came into the room my time with Brandon seemed to cease. I guess this was just how it is between older and younger brothers, you know, rivals for others' attention or affection or whatever, but when my brother came into the room I was teased mercifully by them...and I thought Brandon loved me. This of course further confused me, but I guess that's the way it goes sometimes.

Let me tell you about my grandpa. He was living with my grandma in Omaha. My grandpa was great. I didn't really get to see him a whole lot because of my dad being military, but from what I saw of him and the times we spent together, that was heaven to me.

One day after it had snowed in Omaha, my grandpa gave me a shovel to shovel the walk, or maybe since I was so young he just wanted to appease me because I wanted to help shovel that walk, my family was helping after all. He had given me the shovel and I was about to shovel my first walk, at about age eight or nine...fun time for me with Grandpa, who cares if others were around. I took the shovel in my hand, looked down at the driveway and saw that it was covered in ice. I knew what I had to do. I turned the shovel so the big part, real technical name for it huh, was turned around so I could break the ice with it and I shoved down with all my might, but I didn't hit the ice at all...I hit my foot. I don't know if you've ever hit your foot with a big steel shovel with all your might behind it, as much might as a nine-year-old could have, but it doesn't feel very good. What was strange to me was the fact that I didn't feel any pain. I didn't feel any pain because, of course, the temperature outside was SOOO cold that my feet were frozen, I mean this was Omaha in the winter, right? It had to be several degrees below freezing. Let me tell you people one thing...when that frozen foot sensation wore off...BOY, DID I FEEL IT.

I remember my first night with my grandparents when we first drove up in our little station wagon. We had just come from overseas for a short visit, but when we walked into the front room I felt a great sense of warmth. I loved my grandparents with all my heart. My gamma had this mole or something on her forehead and I still can recall to this very day climbing up on her lap and pressing that little spot on her forehead saying, "Ding dong." My grandma just laughed and cuddled me tighter...there is NOTHING in the world like my grandma's hugs.

When I was in Omaha visiting my grandparents just before or after I went to Germany, I don't remember which (it's funny how sometimes you can remember exactly WHAT happened, but you can't exactly pinpoint a date, and then at other times you can pinpoint a certain date that something happened but your mind just won't let you remember the thing for whatever reason), along with that walk shoveling experience I also had a very weird, but later on very profound, experience with my brother.

It was very late at night, well not really but late for a young kid, and I was fast asleep. My brother and I were in a room with two beds side-by-side and I was in the bed to the right. I was technically not exactly asleep because I saw the door open just a little. My brother was older so of course he got to stay up later then me, therefore, it was obviously him coming into the room to go to sleep...or so I thought.

He came over to my bed and quietly whispered, "Brad, wake up, I'm going to run away."

I was groggy at this point so I had no idea what he was saying except for the 'I'm going' part. I made a point of telling him that if he was going anywhere, I was going to go with him; I mean to me it was just a big adventure and I wanted to be a part of it because I thought we were eventually going to come back...to this day I don't know why I said that.

This time my brother said, "Brad, come with me, we're leaving."

I can recall thinking, *Why are we leaving because I love this place and my grandparents and I don't really want to leave*. But I went with him anyway...he was my brother after all AND older so obviously he knew what he was talking about, right?

We snuck out of our beds, he helped me put my shoes on because even at that age I still couldn't tie my shoes...I have Velcro shoes to this very day, and down the stairs to the garage. The house had an automatic garage door opener so he had to have known that it was going to make a noise when we opened and closed it, but all that mattered to him was getting out of there and, for some reason, not coming back.

When we got to the garage door opener controls he decided it was time to give me the getaway instructions. He told me that he was going to press the button to open the garage door, he actually used those words like I was some kind of eight-year-old simpleton, and allow me to run out the door. Then he was going to press the button again and run REALLY fast out the door before it closed...nice of him to think of my grandparents and want to close the door, huh? It also showed a bit of manners I guess; you know, that whole close the door behind you thing.

He pressed the button to open the door; it made a VERY loud

noise while it was opening up, and I thought of course someone would find us before the door even got open. However, I made my run to the outside of the house.

At this time I was very much into the adventure of it all so waved to him and whispered, "Come on, come on."

He pressed the button and the garage door was going down way too fast and I thought he was going to be left inside and here I would be standing outside in the freezing cold.

He shocked me, however, because just before the garage door looked like it was about to hit the ground he rolled underneath it. I thought that was so awesome that he just rolled under the door like that. I thought, only for a little bit, that he was some kind of stunt boy or something because what he did was so cool.

Now my brother and me were both outside, the garage door was back down and we were free to go anywhere we wanted, but where was that going to be? I let my 'experienced' brother lead the way.

We ran for what seemed like forever and then we walked the rest of the way. I had no idea where we were going, and to tell the truth I don't think my brother had a clue either; we ended up at this place called Boystown. Boystown to me seemed like a cool place because it was bunches and bunches of little apartments that had cool people living there.

We went up to an apartment and walked inside, my brother said that when we went in we were supposed to use fake names. We sat down at this little breakfast nook while some woman that was in the little kitchenette was preparing food or something. I remember she asked me if I wanted anything, and I said I wanted an apple. She gave me an apple and my brother something else and that's when the grilling started. She asked me my name...big mistake. I wasn't known for being a good liar and my brother knew this so when she asked me my brother kind of just stared at me with these 'don't you dare tell her' eyes. I did eventually let my name slip out of my mouth and then I immediately walked out of the room REALLY FAST.

I went into the other room while my brother was left talking to the lady, thank God I was done answering the question and I could be free just to be me and explore my new surroundings.

When I walked into that other room I saw some girl sitting on a couch in the middle of the room staring at a TV in the corner. I saw a movie on the TV, it was long enough to be a movie I thought, and it was VERY scary to me. The movie had zombies dancing and rising from the dead, coming out of crypts with blood and guts everywhere. This movie was the scariest movie I had ever seen in my life. The movie was odd to me as well because it had music with it in the background, but later on it would become a VERY important factor in my life, but for now it was just haunting me. I knew I wanted to get out of there quick and go back to the safe haven of my grandparents house, NEVER to return to this one.

A little later on that night we were walking again because I had already said too much to that lady just by telling her my name. While we were out walking a police car came up behind us (I guess the lady phoned in and ratted us out) and took us away. We were actually picked up by the sheriff of the whole police department. The reason why we were picked up by the sheriff wasn't because we were some high-profile case or anything like that...the sheriff happened to be my mom's brother.

When we got into the sheriff's police car we were taken straight home, no stops downtown for adventure boy. When we got home everybody was up waiting for us, thank God my dad was away doing military stuff or it would have been harder on us than it turned out to be.

I don't remember anyone else's reaction to us having had a night out like we did, but I do remember my grandfather's reaction. My grandfather gave us one of his notorious 'choke talks'. A choke talk isn't really a violent thing; it is just a scare tactic…IT WORKS, BELIEVE ME. My grandfather would begin to talk to us in a calm polite manner and then begin raising his voice. He would at this point cup his hand and place it around our necks like he was going to choke us if we didn't heed his warnings. After that situation we never ran away again; I'd like to think it's because we knew better, but it was probably out of fear of grandpa and the 'choke talk'.

Getting back to my T-ball coach, it was fun just to be around him and his family. I can recall a time when my sister and I went down to the bottom of the stairwell and she taught my coach's son and me how to roller skate…fun times.

They had little stairwell houses where we were staying on the base. The stairwells may have been called something else, but I can only remember calling them stairwells. They were nice little apartments, but that's all they were to me: nice little stairwell apartments.

The most fun I had in that stairwell apartment was ironically also a day I got hurt. I had just fixed myself a bowl of hot grape nuts cereal, not just the cereal with milk in it heated up, but I had maple syrup and brown sugar and honey in mine...it was SOO good and for some reason to this day I can't duplicate that recipe. I had just fixed a bowl for myself (actually my mom made it earlier and I just spooned it into my bowl...I wasn't a good cook back then and I'm still not because I live out of the microwave basically), when I heard this commotion from downstairs. I was on my way, with bowl in hand, down the stairwell to find out what was going on. I guess I went out the door too quickly because I remember whipping around REAL fast at the top of the stairwell. The next thing I knew I tripped and I fell, the bowl flying with me, down two flights of stairs. All the contents of my hot cereal were still in the bowl. That was the funniest thing I'd ever done in my entire life, I overcame the pain real quick because I was laughing so hard.

I never really felt at home in that little stairwell apartment because being a military brat, as any military kid was called, we were always moving around so much and from that I never really got used to being anyplace for long, it was kind of adventurous. That's what life is SUPPOSED to be about, being young and having fun...little did I know that Germany was going to be famous to me for more than just fun.

I remember going to elementary school there too and being in this VERY NICE lady's class, I can't remember her name, but I can remember that she was a very nice lady. Oh Yeah, the nice lady's name was Mrs. McDonald. I remember that now because I used to laugh at that a lot. I laughed at the name for obvious reasons, I mean old McDonald's farm and the McDonald's restaurant food chain...God if I was only the funny person back then that I like to think I am now, I would have made so many jokes and probably gotten into so much trouble.

They had fluoride in the water in Germany back then, I don't recall if they did that here in the states. I can't remember if it was every other day or every week, but this nurse, or whomever the heck he or she was, would come into the classroom with this BIG silver looking canister, it looked like it could have tea or soda in it, wishful thinking from an elementary school student who KNEW that wasn't what it was. Beside the big silver canister were lots of little itty-bitty cups. The student who was assigned to pass the cups out would pick up a handful of these itty-bitty cups and place one in front of every student. The person, because I can't remember if it was a he or a she (give me a break it was at least twenty-two years ago), who was in charge of the large canister would then go to each individual person and you had to hold out your cup and they would fill it, not full, with this blue liquid.

When this person was wheeling this cart around with this canister on it, several questions went through my mind. Why had they given us such little cups if it was something we were supposed to drink? How come the cups weren't being filled all the way? What was that mysterious blue liquid?

We were all supposed to wait until everybody got theirs before we could drink it. I thought to myself, *Why do I have to wait for everybody else?* We all got our little cups with our little blue liquid, which looked like Kool-Aid to me, and we were ready to have our drink. The teacher told us while the drink was getting passed around that when we put it in our mouths we weren't supposed to swallow it, we were supposed to swish it around in our mouths and then spit it back into the cup. I thought this was VERY strange, but I just chalked it up to being in a foreign country, even though it was on a US military base. When the teacher said go and I put the liquid into my mouth, I made the most horrific face I bet that any little kid had ever made. I didn't know they were going to do that to me. How could they put these little kids through that torture EVERY WEEK? It was simply inhuman. I never put my cup out there again...unless the teacher made me.

I also want to tell you about this incident, I shouldn't call it that because it makes you think that I did something wrong I bet...which I didn't think I did. I want to tell you about this 'trip' I went on to a place called the Black Forest, which was ironically also in Germany. I don't remember much about that trip at all. What I do remember is getting on the bus to go there and getting off the bus when we got there. I can also recall when I was there walking into a store, it wasn't like any store we have over here in the states. This particular store, or whatever it was called, looked just like a house. If you can picture the gingerbread house from the fairy tale, that's exactly what it looked like to me...what can I say? I was nine and had a very imaginative mind.

I went into this gingerbread-house-looking store and I wanted to buy something nice for my teacher because I naively thought she had paid for all of us to come here. I didn't know that the school paid for it or I might not have bought her anything...who am I kidding? Of course I would have bought her something...I'm such a suckup. I went into the store and I found this cherry drink that I thought she might enjoy because I LOVED cherry drinks; I thought cherries tasted soo good. I thought it was just a regular cherry drink, but apparently it had alcohol in it. How was I supposed to know that they could sell alcohol to minors over there? She looked at the bottle and her eyes met mine, but she didn't have quite the same reaction that I did or that I was looking for. Needless to say she was a little miffed. I don't know whether she was miffed at me for buying alcohol or she was miffed at the store for selling it to me. Since living on military bases was all I knew, I wasn't as worldly as she was.

There was also a time in elementary school, in that same woman's class, that I and another girl had co-won a spelling bee or something...I don't remember exactly what. She paid for both of us, after class no less, to go out with her. Thinking about Mrs. McDonald right now I can tell you she was a VERY refined lady and VERY well-mannered, heck she reminded me of Mary Poppins, she was so prim and proper and didn't let you get away with anything.

She took us out to eat at this very posh, because I don't know any other way to describe it, establishment. I mean there was elevator music and everything. I remember the girl also. I don't remember her name, but I can remember her looks as clear as a bell. If anyone remembers Ms Hathaway from the Beverly Hillbillies then just make that lady about nine years old and you have the very same picture of the girl that went out with Mrs. McDonald and I. If it sounds like I was on a date with Mrs. McDonald, I kind of was. She made me feel so good inside. She corrected me when I was wrong and praised me when I did right...she is one of my main influences in life and I will NEVER forget her. Ok, when I first started talking about her I almost forgot her name, but that's beside the point.

Let's not talk about my teachers for now...let's move on to dangerous territory.

There was a hill, a very steep hill, that all the kids liked to slide down. This hill was called SUICIDE Hill. Imagine if you will, one half of an eggshell. If you can't imagine the eggshell then imagine the letter 'U', but deepen the bottom part and stretch it out a very long way. The eggshell, or the 'U', happened to be named Suicide Hill because it was rumored, of course, that people died on it somehow. I don't remember the legend of it or anything like that; I just remember it was fun to go down it in the snow. Summer on Suicide Hill was cool as well. People would come from all over with their bikes just to ride down the paths of the hill. Personally I didn't see the fun in riding a bike down Suicide Hill, probably because I never learned to ride. My parents never bothered to teach me because of my eye problems…which was ok with me though because I can get along just fine with never learning how to ride.

Winter on Suicide Hill was a much different experience for me. In wintertime Suicide Hill became more to me than a chance to watch people having fun riding their bikes, motorbikes, etc. around, it became time for me to have some fun.

I came down to Suicide Hill one day after it snowed and there wasn't one patch of snow at all…it was all ICE, that was my first indication of why it was called Suicide Hill…because you had to be a crazy person to want be on it. I was very happy going there because I knew it was now MY TIME. No longer would I have to sit there on the top of the hill watching others as they careened down until they reached the bottom and then lug their bikes back up it again only to have more fun going down the second time. No longer would I have to sit in amazement and sadness watching as others did bike tricks down that hill and know that I could never do that. This was MY TIME; this was the time where I could show everybody what I could do.

I got up the very next morning and asked Mom and Dad if I could go out to play down at the hill. My parents were a little concerned about the fact that I wanted to play down there with it being winter and all, and who could blame them? But they said ok.

I got all my snow gear on. You know what I mean, the stuff that makes you invariably look like a mummy when you walk out of the house. You talk like one too because you have masks and things on your face to keep out the cold, and those things are so tight on your face that your voice doesn't even sound like your voice anymore...it sounds like some muffled drunk person's voice.

My parents said I had to go with my brother or sister, I don't remember which one I picked and I don't think it really mattered all that much to me, I just wanted to get down there and have some fun. What I did end up doing when I got down there was far from fun and exciting to a normal person, but for me it was very much a fun experience. I got on my sled, a little flying-saucer-looking sled. I did my little one, two, three motion; you know where you slide your butt and the sled back and forth one, two, three. When I got to number three I let go of the ground I was holding on to and let gravity and the force of my pushing do its thing. I was on my way, sailing down to the bottom. Now I'm a person who doesn't like to work very hard, anyone who's ever tried to make me do chores knows that about me, so when I went sailing down that VERY icy hill at what seemed to be like a thousand miles an hour, to a kid that's how fast it seemed, I was scared out of my wits. I kept thinking all the time that I was going to tip over out of that sled and fall flat on my face...I just didn't want to do that. To make matters worse, after I got done, arms and legs flailing on that sled all the way down that hill, I had to walk all the way back UP again. I knew that once was enough for me and that I NEVER wanted to do that again, where do you think I went the very next week?

Yeah…SUICIDE HILL.

I had very few friends in Germany, but one friend I could always count on was named Jan. Of course, we were both military kids so we knew that our time together was probably short because that happens to all military kids; a crop of kids come and a crop of kids get shipped off with their military parents to someplace else, but that thought NEVER registered with me…I can't speak for Jan. I'm not putting down military families or military life, you see, it's just that when you're a little kid, it's very hard to get shuffled from one place to another every couple of years and have to adjust to new surroundings and new friends, knowing that you have left your old friends behind.

My friend Jan and I did everything together. We would call each other on the phone and make plans for what we were going to do when we got together; he lived quite a way away from me. When we saw each other it was like magic, I've never had another friend like that, and I don't believe I ever will. When we got together it was like there was nobody else around except for him and me.

We had such a blast that when it ended, I was just heartbroken. I remember hearing the news for the first time that my friend Jan wasn't going to be around any longer and that our time had come to an end. We had one last playtime together where he came over and we just played and played like nothing was wrong. It was like everything was right with the world and we were going to be able to stay together forever. It eventually came time for us to say our goodbyes and we, of course, were good little soldiers about it. The door closed with Jan on the outside and me on the inside and I got REAL quiet…deathly quiet.

I went into the other room and got a little piece of paper and a pen. I sat down on the couch with that paper and pen and began writing. The letters I wrote, I wrote VERY slowly, were J...A...N. I wrote those letters down and then I tilted my head very slowly to look at what I had written. At that moment I wasn't conscious of what I was writing, I was just writing instinctively, but when I looked down on the page and saw what I had written and realized that I had written Jan's name...something happened. I'd been good about moving around up until then. I'd accepted that we would be moving from place to place on a regular basis. I hadn't been alive that long so I wasn't moved around a lot, therefore my life was pretty stable, but I had been at this point to Texas, California, and Nebraska...of course the latter two were just visits so I really hadn't been moved around at all when you think about it. I just snapped when I read Jan's name on that piece of paper. I began crying a very guttural cry that I had NEVER heard myself make before. I cried hard and then I began repeating his name out loud over and over again. While I was crying and repeating his name I started tearing up the paper because it was like my heart had been torn out of my chest and somebody had thrown it on the floor, and they were stomping all over it. I never got over it; I still miss Jan to this day and wonder what ever became of him.

I also had another friend whose name was Ian. I will delve into what led my brain to think this way later on in the book, but I thought he was very cute and I wondered all the time what would happen if I just approached him and tried something with him. Ian was quite a different type of friend than Jan was. With Jan I had a friend that came over once in a while because he lived quite a way away, but for the most part we had to stick to phone conversations, with Ian it was a whole different type of friendship.

I got to see Ian anytime I wanted to see him because he lived in the neighborhood. I also had a different relationship with him because of the fact that he was a real big jokester and liked to make people laugh. This was one of my first introductions to that because although I have apparently done some funny things in the past, I wasn't going out of my way to MAKE it funny or to make people laugh. Ian also did this funny thing with his voice which I still can't do to this day, but I'll always remember it because it sounded so hilarious to me.

You know how when you've been outside in the cold for a very long time, or you've been working out or walking in very extreme heat, and then you come inside and you are panting really heavily, that was the beginning of this funny noise that he could make. Ian started out with a real slow pant and then he would make it louder and louder and louder until it was just about the loudest you could make it, and then suddenly that loud panting gave way to a foghorn type noise that had to come from way down deep inside him. I heard him make this noise EVERY time we would meet up. I would practice it so much that I remember hurting myself several times and I still couldn't make this noise at all.

I recall on several occasions we would meet up behind my apartment complex while we were heading to the playground. There were some woods in the back of the apartments that we had to walk through to get to the playground. Well, we didn't really have to walk through the woods because there were the apartments, then this big open field and the woods after that. We would walk through the big open field between the apartment complex and the woods that went all the way down to our playground area. While we were walking towards the playground one day (I don't know whether he said it just to scare me or whether he actually thought it was real), Ian told me about this monster that lived in those woods that liked to grab little children and eat them up. He described this monster as; well if you've ever seen the show *Harry and the Hendersons* then you know what I'm talking about, a grotesque looking beast. I looked over into the woods as he was telling me the story and I could swear I saw the monster moving around in there. Several times I actually braved that walk on my own and went down to the woods just far enough before properly going into them...I never did actually go into the woods.

There was another friend I had in Germany and he was VERY influential to me, but for some reason I can't remember the boy's name...sounds influential, doesn't it? He was one of my best friends because I could tell that he really loved me as a person. The most important thing that I remember him for was a very small gesture, but I will never forget it. I was at home watching TV or bugging my mom, or something like that, when the phone rang. My mom picked it up and it was this kid. My mom handed me the phone and this kid said he wanted me to come down to his house so we could play. The fact that ANY person actually wanted me in their house knowing what I looked like was a great boost for me. Not only was it not just somebody that wanted me to come down, it was someone my age that wanted me to come down be with them. I don't remember anything else about this person, it is said that some people only remember the good stuff, it is said that some people only remember the bad stuff...I remember the important stuff.

There were several people in our stairwell that I was close to. I was kind of friends with this boy on the bottom of the stairwell whose name I also don't remember. However, I do remember that when I rang his doorbell and he answered he ALWAYS had a cup of yogurt in his hand and a spoon in his mouth...he made me laugh because he would always do that spoon on the end of the nose trick...still gets me every time when I see that from somebody. I think his mom and dad both worked because they were never home when I went there; he was always alone.

There was also this boy in the apartment above us named Eric Stemerling. Eric lived with his mom and dad and two sisters, Kristi, and I forgot the other one's name. I think at least one of the sisters was a stepsister to Eric but I never did ask.

One day Eric and I went up to the very top of the stairwell, which was kind of the attic to the complex, you didn't have to open it like you do in attics in a home; you just kind of opened the door and went in. We went up to the attic and found a whole bunch of boxes, but he kind of gravitated me towards this box that was hiding in the corner. We opened the box and inside was this bunch of dirty magazines. They were some Playboys, and some that were definitely not Playboys. I definitely wanted to look at the ones that weren't Playboys because they weren't 'posed' like the Playboys were; they were in positions that looked like if you moved half an inch one way or the other you could wind up in the hospital. Eric showed me these magazines, for what reason I don't know... perhaps because it was that 'oh we're doing something we're not supposed to do' kind of thing, but I've got to tell you, I was getting turned on big time. I wasn't getting turned on because the girls in the magazine were showing all of their stuff, I was getting turned on because I wanted Eric to take the hint and show me all of his stuff.

Eric was a blond-haired, blue-eyed, very sexy boy, and I wanted him. Eric had absolutely no idea that I was attracted to him. I wasn't really 'attracted' to him in the sense of the word that grownups think; I wanted his body, and that was all that I wanted. I found myself doing anything and everything I could just to be able to touch him. It wasn't all about just ripping his clothes off and having my way with him though, I enjoyed being with him as well. He had this huge white dog he called Snowflake. He wasn't lying when he named this dog Snowflake; she really looked like a big white furball. He would come to get me from my apartment sometimes when he had to take Snowflake for a walk and we would just talk and talk about anything, and sometimes nothing made sense...kind of like Kramer on *Seinfeld*.

We had a cat in that stairwell apartment which I will never forget. We didn't have that cat for a very long time as I recall, but she definitely provided a memorable moment. Her name was Princess, and she definitely lived up to that name for me; I loved that cat so much that I would always cuddle up next to her and play with her...she was more than a pet to me at times.

One day we were all inside and talking or doing something, and I don't know how she got out there, but she was out on the ledge of the balcony of our apartment, and we were about three stories up. We heard a noise coming from the balcony and we all looked up in time to see Princess diving off of it. We all raced down the stairs to see if she was ok, which she was, but when we got her back up to the safe haven of our apartment we noticed that she had busted her nose wide open. There was this beautiful cat who now had a little piece of her nose chipped off. It was red underneath so all you saw when you looked at her straight on was a little red speck that for some reason never went away. It served her right for trying to be a daredevil cat...I miss her.

I will never forget one day when Eric and I were walking Snowflake, something happened that never should have taken place. There were these other tenants in the building we lived in who I didn't particularly care for at all. I don't remember if it was a whole family or not, but I know there was a dad and a little girl. The dad came out of the complex, my brother was out there with Eric and I, and he just came right smack dab up to my brother, who was no more than twelve or thirteen at the time, and shoved him to the ground for, what appeared to me, no reason at all. Snowflake had just done her business, number two, and this man held my brother's face down to it. I don't remember at all what was being said, but I do remember there was snow and dog shit on the ground. The man's hand was forcefully holding my brother's head down to the crap on the ground and was slowly inching his head forwards into it. My brother's nose was inching ever closer to that crap and I could hear the guy saying, "Can you smell it?" and other things to that effect.

I remember being so frightened and scared of this man that I didn't dare do anything because the same fate, or worse, might happen to me. At the same time I was scared for myself I was also scared for my brother and angry with this man for treating him this way. When it was all over, and I don't remember what stopped it, I remember my brother being very pissed off and he said he was going to kill that guy...unfortunately that never did happen.

There was this friend of Eric's named Chris; I've forgotten his last name, who fronted being my friend. What I mean by 'fronted' is basically that he faked being my friend just so Eric would like him better because Eric was my friend...hey we were real young and immature at that age. Chris was an oriental looking kid and to me he was very cute. When I got introduced to him by Eric I couldn't believe my luck, here was this sexy friend of mine who knew this cute boy who also wanted to be my friend…my frame of mind was geared toward something else back then (you'll find out why) or else I would have smelled that something wasn't right.

One day Chris called me on the phone and asked if I would come over to his house and that Eric was there with him or was on his way over, it's kind of fuzzy; I was very happy that he asked me. I went over to his house and Eric wasn't there so I asked what was going on, I've forgotten what he said. Chris then heard the doorbell ring and his mom said it was Eric. Chris asked me to hide under the bed. I asked him why, but he just told me to hide. I relented and hid under the bed; hey, when somebody that cute tells you to do something, you just do it.

Eric came in the room and they both started talking, but then someone said something and I came out from under the bed and confronted them. Eric and Chris both ordered me out of the house…I don't recall ever going back to Chris's house again or ever being his friend again…for some odd reason I was still Eric's friend, probably, and I hate to say this, because of the way he looked.

My brother had a friend named Mickey, who happened to be in the Boy Scouts; this leads me into the very first time I remember being afraid of my brother. My brother and I had left the house and gone over to Mickey's house. Mickey was wearing his Boy Scouts uniform so I thought maybe we were going to take him to a Boy Scout meeting or something like that…how wrong I was; we went somewhere all right, but it wasn't to any Boy Scout meeting.

We picked the uniformed Mickey up from his house and we were on our way. As we walked down the street from his house I had no idea where we were headed or how long it would take us to get there, I was just happy to go along for the ride with my brother and his friend.

My brother and his friend were, of course, older than I was so the fact that they wanted to hang out with me, even for a brief walk I thought, was the greatest thing to ever happen to me. I looked up to my brother and idolized him somewhat. I knew I could never be what he was, which was a person who had 20/20 vision and walked perfectly without bumping into things, so to be in the presence of that was a pretty awesome thing for a kid like me.

As we walked further along the sidewalk I began to think to myself that I knew this area, which I shouldn't have because we were supposed to be going somewhere I'd never been before. We had ended up back in our neighborhood because I recognized all the white apartment buildings, so I had NO CLUE what was going on or what was about to happen. Mickey's house may have been an apartment building like ours was, but it sure didn't look like it from the outside...so for me, we weren't anywhere close to where we lived and that was great because it was like a little adventure for me.

There we were, back in our neighborhood and I was just walking along with them oblivious to what was about to happen. We ended up at the little playground. I was so excited because, first, it meant that we weren't where we were supposed to be I thought...so that added a bit of thrill to this adventure. Secondly, I thought that since we were at the playground my brother and Mickey wanted to play with me. I thought it was so awesome that they wanted to not just walk with me somewhere but actually to play with them and let me be a part of their activities...even if it was just for that one day, that's all I ever wanted.

The playground was a place for younger kids AND older kids because it had EVERYTHING. This playground had a large open field for anyone who wanted to play football or just basically run around in it. Up the hill from the open field, which I remember always had tall grass you could get lost in, was a big open area with a layer of dirt on the ground like you would see on a baseball field. In that open area with the layer of dirt they had a little sandbox for the little children to play in, the rest of the area was for the 'grownups', the older children basically. It had a massive tire swing. I don't know if any of you have ever seen tire swings before, but it was an awesome sight to see, and even greater looking with people playing on it.

Picture if you will a large piece of wood about the size of a small picnic table sticking up out of the ground, and another slightly shorter one on top of it and slanted inwards. On the bottom part of the board slanted inwards, up at the top, were two boards crisscrossing each other. Hanging down from the two crisscrossed boards were four chains. Attached to these four chains was a tire lying flat and corked in the middle with a huge piece of round wood...that was our tire swing.

The tire swing was a cool sight to see, but like I said, it was better when you saw someone swinging from it. Sometimes one person would get on one side of it and wrap their hands around the steel chains on either side and try to rock it back and forth, but it looked very awkward and not much fun at all. Most of the time what you would see was one person getting on one side and another person getting on the opposite. They would fasten both of their hands around the two steel chains that they had on either side of them, and then they would both seesaw back and forth and try to see how high they could get. Several times I'd seen people actually go all the way around, and then of course to add more danger to it they would go as high as they could and then jump off. At times two people would get on opposite sides of the tire swing and fasten their hands around the steel chains and then ask if anybody wanted to sit in the middle, don't forget that there was that wooden board in the middle. People would always say no at first, but then get coaxed into sitting in the middle while the others were pumping as hard as they could to get the swing to go as high as it could and then they would jump off, leaving the person in the middle just sitting there enjoying the ride. One time, and only one time, it was me in the middle...I had snow-white knuckles at the end of that ride.

When Mickey, my brother, and I got to the park they wasted no time in heading to the tire swing. I was the slow one, but when I arrived they asked me to get on it and they would get on either side and pump it so that I would have a nice fun ride. I knew from previous experience that it was NOT a nice fun ride, at least not in my eyes, and I was never getting on that thing again. My brother finally relented because I told him I was never getting on that thing, and I also told him why I was never getting on that tire swing ever again. My brother came up with the next best thing.

My brother told me to hold on to the swing and he would spin me around while I was sitting in the middle of it, I thought that would be a fun idea. I hopped in the middle of the tire and my brother and Mickey, who were on it because they were getting ready to pump it back and forth like a swing, got off. My brother spun that thing around so fast that I thought I was going to become dizzy and throw up or something...but it was fun.

My brother then told me to get off, which I did. My hands were still holding on to the thick heavy steel chains when something unexpected happened. I saw at that point in time my brother, whom I loved so much and I would have done anything for if I could, look up at Mickey and give him a little nod of his head as if to say 'do it'. I saw Mickey's hand go into his pocket and come out with something, but it was done so fast that I didn't get a chance to see what it was before I figured out that I was in trouble. I all of a sudden felt my wrists getting closer to the steel chains…closer than I had ever wanted them to get. I looked down at my wrists and I realized that the reason they were closer to the chains was because Mickey, when my brother had given him the nod, had pulled handcuffs out of his pocket and had handcuffed my wrists to the chains.

With my wrists handcuffed securely to two of the four heavy steel chains, one of them got off of the tire swing, I forget now which one, and spun it around as hard as he could. He then got back up onto the tire swing and just watched what was going to happen next.

The swing was going around REAL fast, fast for a kid my age anyway, and I was trying to hold on for dear life as this thing ran around in circles. I knew I couldn't just let go of the swing because my wrists were handcuffed to it so there was no way of getting off. I knew I couldn't just stop myself because this thing was going around way too fast, and if I was to just stop myself I knew something ugly would happen. There I was running as fast as I could around and around and it seemed I would never be able to stop. In reality I only went around about half a turn, then I couldn't run anymore and my feet just stopped. My body was dragging for about half a turn when Mickey finally jumped off and decided he had seen enough and abruptly stopped the tire from spinning any more.

I was crying so heavily at this point in time because not only had it hurt physically, but it also hurt emotionally because, even though I didn't know what Mickey was like, I couldn't believe my very own brother, a person who I basically idolized, could do this to me and put me through so much pain.

Mickey jumped off the tire swing and uncuffed my wrists from the chains. I looked down at my wrists and I saw where the skin had been taken off. My skin wasn't just taken off where the cuffs were originally put on my wrists because apparently they weren't put on tight enough...thank God or they might have drawn blood, the skin was taken off of several different places on my lower arm.

The handcuffs were taken off me and I was left there sitting on the ground sobbing horribly. I could hear Mickey telling me he was sorry for what he had done. I wasn't concerned at all that Mickey was sorry for what he had done because I didn't care about him, I had just one thought in my mind and that thought was to my brother...WHY?

I looked up through a tear-stained face at my brother, the perpetrator of this crime, and when I tilted my head all the way up so I could look him straight in the eye...I saw SATAN. My brother had the biggest Cheshire cat grin on his face that I had ever seen in my life. Not only did he have a big grin on his face, but this grin was also accompanied by laughter. I'd heard my brother laugh before, but this laughter was unlike anything I had ever heard in my short lifetime. The way he looked down at me as I was lying there sobbing with tears running down my face wasn't a look of 'oh we're just having fun and didn't mean to cause any pain'...he MEANT to cause me pain. The way he laughed his little demonic laugh was so frightening to me that I remember for the first time in my life having fear in my heart when it came to my brother.

CHAPTER 3:
SEXUAL ESCAPADES

This is it; this is the meat and potatoes, or the center of this whole book. This is the part of the book that the sickos and sexually deviants will immediately turn to when they find the chapter name after purchasing this book. Maybe they won't even purchase this book. Maybe they are looking at these pages in the store right now. Maybe they have this book in their grubby little hands and they are now looking from side to side to see if anyone is watching them reading this chapter. If this happens to be you who are reading this chapter while in the store...PUT THE BOOK DOWN or buy it.

My first sexual experience happened when I was five years old, ironically it was my ONLY heterosexual encounter, it happened during my first visit to Texas. I was in this strange woman's class, her name was Mrs. Raiyna, I believe that's how you spell her name, I was only five and it was 1980...at this point I could probably barely spell my own name.

The reason I call her strange is that one day I got her mad and she told me, "Do you want to see a little boy fly without wings?" but I knew she was cool just from that statement. Her school, look at the way I said that...it wasn't really HER school, I mean it's not as if she owned it. The school was called The Little Red Schoolhouse. To me it resembled a barn from the outside; I expected little farm animals to come out of that place. My first sexual encounter happened in The Little Red Schoolhouse.

Her name was Jennifer. I don't remember much about the way she looked because it happened so long ago. The truth is more likely that I don't remember what she looked like because her looks didn't make or have that big of an impact in my life. No matter how long it has been, if something or someone makes a huge impact in your life, you WILL remember. I do, however, remember what we did.

It was a day just like any other day. I came in to the schoolroom and sat down at my desk. My teacher was passing out a test, it's been so long of course I don't remember what the test was about, and we had the rest of class to complete it. Jennifer and I were sitting side by side. We started taking the test and then something very strange happened. Jennifer started looking over at me and then looking down at her paper in a back and forth type of motion. I didn't know what was going on, I thought maybe she wanted me to give her the answers to the test or something like that. I tell you one thing, however, I wasn't about to cheat for anybody; no siree. It turned out that she wasn't looking at her paper at all. In one motion this little five-year-old girl that I hadn't known for very long took her free hand that was dangling under her desk and put it on my hand that was also dangling under my desk. I was five and very naive about things, but I mean come on, I knew something was happening. Little did I know just how far she would take it though.

As I was saying, she put her hand on my hand underneath MY desk. Strangely enough, this was ok with me, I mean I had no idea what she was going to do next, let alone what the ramifications would be later on so I just let her put her hand on my hand under my desk. What she did next shocked me so much because I was totally unprepared. This sweet little innocent young girl named Jennifer took my hand from underneath my desk and with a very swift motion, so others couldn't see what she was doing I assumed, she moved both our hands underneath her desk. She next did something so bizarre that I think for a little bit there my body must have gone into shock because I couldn't move a muscle. She took my hand, which was underneath hers, and she put it over her vagina. I didn't know what to do. I was shocked. She let her hand rest a little bit on my hand, which happened to be over her vagina. She let it rest there for what seemed to me to be like an eternity. She began to move my hand with her hand in an up and down motion, I was still a little terrified at this moment because she was doing EVERYTHING...I was basically frozen in my chair.

After a while I wasn't frozen anymore and I began to pick up on what she was doing, so then I continued rubbing her on my own because she had removed her hand. I was pretty comfortable with what was going on at this point in time because I knew what she wanted me to do, so I just kept doing it...until she surprised me again. Jennifer had taken her hand away from mine and I thought that would be the end of it; you know, I would just continue rubbing her for a while and then somehow it would just stop...either maybe I would get caught or the bell would ring or something like that would happen and it would be over, I was wrong. She had taken her hand away from being on top of my hand for a purpose which I found out soon enough.

She had looked over at me while my hand was rubbing her as if to say 'do you like what you are doing?' and I looked back at her with a look that was kind of like saying 'it's not bad'. She looked at me again with this kind of 'are you ready?' look in her eyes and then she reciprocated what I was doing to her. Jennifer took her free hand, the other one had to look like it was still taking the test I guess, and put it underneath my desk. I kind of knew what was about to happen at this point, but the fact that she went ahead and did what she did just totally weirded me out.

She took her free hand that was underneath my desk and put it inside my pants. I didn't have my hand on top of hers like she had on mine, but she seemed like she needed no help and knew exactly what she was doing. Jennifer then began rubbing my penis. I'm sure many of us have had our penis rubbed before by girls and it feels good to us, but at the age of five, I've got to tell you, it just felt plain weird to me. We sat there basically taking the test and rubbing each other for what seemed like hours…in reality it wasn't that long at all because class was over before we knew it.

I don't remember anything bad ever happening as a result of what we had done. I don't remember any punishment for being caught or any other repercussions. I also don't remember anything like that ever happening again between Jennifer and me. I will always remember that moment fondly because although it was a very sexually charged moment, well, as sexually charged as you can get at the age of five, it was a very sweet and tender moment for me. I don't remember it being a sexual moment like two little sexual deviant five years old who just want to get off on the feelings that that kind of behavior can cause. I remember it as being a moment of discovery like a little baby would discover his toes or fingers and stick them in his or her mouth. It was a very sweet, and admittedly shocking, moment to me back then and it is a very sweet moment to me now; I will always remember that moment exactly for what it was. This moment in my life would also prepare me a little for what came next.

I don't remember exactly when I met Bubba and Telly, but I do know that they changed my life, and my way of thinking, forever.

Telly was a black boy, boy of color, African American...I don't really know what to say here because I don't want to offend. Bubba was an as sweet as can be southern boy with that southern drawl, and I think the way he talked was why he got away with as much as he did.

They weren't really friends of mine; we just sort of hung out together sometimes. I know I must have met them at school because I'm not the type of person who would go out and play on his own, just meet up with somebody and then they would be my friend...I'm not even that way today. Don't get me wrong, I mean at work or other places I happen to be I will strike up friendships if the opportunity presents itself, but I will not go out of my way to just take a walk out somewhere in the hopes of talking to someone and making new friends. I had a VERY strange relationship with these two boys.

Yes, Telly and Bubba were their real names, as far as I can tell, but that is where the REAL ended in our friendship/relationship. Everything else knew about them was fake and built on lies. Oh yes, I thought I had a real friendship going with these two, but it turned out that we were ALL using each other for gratification purposes and we really didn't know anything about one another the way real friends should.

I remember a lot about being with Bubba and Telly. I remember going over to Bubba's house several times thinking how him and I were going to play together, but when I got there Telly was there as well and we did play together, but not how I thought we would. I don't remember how our sick relationship started, but I will never ever be able to erase from my mind the things that we did together. Most people will call what we did together experimenting because of our ages, I was only six at the time, but I know for a fact it was way more than experimenting.

One day, Bubba, Telly and I were in school, it was during a lunch period or something, and we all went into the bathroom together. I remember being the fall guy so to speak because we went there under the pretense that I didn't know how to tie my shoes, which I really didn't, and they were going to help me tie them. Once we got into that stall and locked the door Bubba pulled his pants down. Bubba then instructed me to suck his dick; at that point in time a whole lot of emotions went through my mind all at once. The first thought that went through my mind was that I hoped we didn't get caught by anyone. The second thought was that this felt different than what I had done with Jennifer. The third thought that was going through my head was that this felt good to me, but when was it going to be my turn?

If I knew then what I know now situations and feelings on my part would have been a whole lot different. I thought to myself that he must be older than us because we had teeny-weeny ones, but his was quite big for a five or six-year-old boy.

It was like five or ten minutes that I did this to Bubba, I remember that whenever anybody sucked him off we always did it longer, but when he did it, it didn't last very long...just an observation, and then it was Telly's turn to do this to Bubba. I can remember not even thinking that it was weird that I was here sucking a boy's dick and there was someone watching me.

Then it was my turn to sit on the toilet, for some reason that's where we sat down in there, and get this done to me. First it was Bubba's turn to do this to me. What was weird about it was the fact that I just sat there like a robot and didn't really feel anything...practically no emotions went through me at all except I hope we don't get caught. Then it was Telly's turn to do this to me and it was like my whole attitude changed. When he started to do it a feeling came over me of sheer ecstasy that I cannot describe. It was so weird to me that Bubba had done this to me and I felt absolutely nothing, but the moment Telly started doing it I never wanted him to stop. From that experience I will take away a couple of different thoughts. Whenever I taste or smell maple syrup I will always think of Bubba because to me that is what he tasted like. When I think of cobwebs I will think of Telly because, although I've never tasted a cobweb before, to me he just had that dry kind of no taste. We had many more experiences that weren't in a school toilet, but they were equally as strange to me.

One day, Bubba, Telly and I were walking home from school, I guess about this time we had crossed that threshold into being something more than suck-off buddies...boy was I wrong. We were all three walking home from school when all of a sudden Bubba wanted us to stop, so we did. I guess Bubba was like the leader of our so-called group and whatever he said to do we just did without question...that's as close to peer pressure as I got. All three of us stopped and we gathered behind this shrub that was in front of a house in our neighborhood, we then took turns sucking each other off right then and there. I can't believe that no one caught us because it's not like we were well hidden, I mean we weren't out in the absolute open or anything because we were behind a bush so it was somewhat dark in that area, but we weren't exactly hidden from all view. I remember getting somewhat of a rush from that because we could have gotten caught at any moment. I didn't think we were doing anything BAD mind you, but I did think others would find it a little bit questionable.

After we had 'done our thing' behind the bush, Bubba asked us if we wanted to go to his house, Telly and I both said sure so we pulled up our pants and went to Bubba's house. When we got there I remember going to his room and him shutting his door. When Bubba shut his door we all continued more of the same of what we had been doing behind that bush. My pants were all the way down at this point in time and I heard a knock on Bubba's door. Bubba went over to open the door and I was pleading with him not to open it yet because my pants weren't all the way up, but he proceeded to open it anyway. Thank God I was able to get them up in time...I was so embarrassed at that moment that he wouldn't care if my pants were all the way down or not, he just went to the door and threw it open like everything was normal.

Way back in 1980 I had no idea what sexual experimentation was, but now that I know what it is I can honestly tell you that I never had any sexual experimentation because what we did together went WAY beyond that. I'd have to say that Bubba and Telly were two of the most influential people in my life because I will never forget the time I was with them...you might say that it colored my whole life.

There was one particular day that I will never forget. I don't recall whether it was when I was in Texas the first time in 1980-83, or when I was in Germany from 83-86, but I will never ever forget what happened on that day because it is burned into my memory, and it is one of the reasons that I never told my dad about anything that was going on in my life.

I had a 'friend' come over one day and we went to my room, shut the door, and played a couple games. We were playing for a little while and he said, "I dare you to get naked." So I did. To this day I don't know why I did it because usually when someone dares you, there has to be something on the line, right? There wasn't.

There I was sitting in front of this boy totally naked. Then he took a piece from this board game that we had out and said to me, "I dare you to stick this up your butt." Don't ask me what compelled me to do it, but I was on my way to accomplishing that when there was a knock on the door.

I didn't get up to answer the door, for obvious reasons, but the door opened anyhow. I was struggling so hard to find my pants that were all the way on the floor, we were on the top bunk of bunk beds that my mom and dad had bought for my brother and I, but I didn't get there in time before the door opened all the way. There this boy and I were, sitting on the top bunk, him fully clothed and me totally naked, when who should walk through my bedroom door…my father. I don't remember seeing anger register on my father's face, but boy did that other kid run out of the room real fast.

I was sitting there totally naked with my father staring right at me and wondering what he was going to do…I didn't have to wonder for long. My father took off his black belt, that's just the color he happened to wear…he wasn't into karate or anything, and proceeded to whip me with it. I know now that fathers spank their children out of love and it is also supposed to teach that child not to repeat that behavior, but DAMN that hurt. I could also feel the buckle of the belt as it dug into my skin, he probably didn't mean for that to happen because I don't think loving and caring fathers ever want to… like… kill their children, and it left marks not only on my skin. It also left marks in my mind because, as I've said previously, I've never told him any other really bad thing that I have done because I didn't want the punishment that I was going to have to face...in retrospect that decision has probably caused me more harm than good.

There was a time in Germany that I remember vividly. I think I remember it because of the fact that it was the ONLY sexual encounter that I ever had in Germany. I had sexual feelings while I was there; I mean there was Eric and Chris, but only one sexual situation where I actually did anything with another person.

This encounter happened when we were living in those little stairwell apartments. I was great friends with the Maldonado family, and especially with their youngest son, Michael. There were three stairwell apartment buildings side by side and we were living in building number one, I call it that because that's the first one I got to when I got home from school, and they were living in building number three.

I would go into the back of building number three sometimes and I would peek down into the basement. I would see little red curtains on the windows so you couldn't see in to see what was going on, the way my mind was working back then I thought that there was something sexual going on in that basement and I wanted to get down there and see what was happening for myself.

One day I got led down to that basement by a couple of boys in the Maldonado family, by this time I was very good friends with them so I guess they felt they could trust me, and I saw something I wasn't prepared to see when I got there. When I got down to the basement I looked up at the windows, and I saw those little red curtains that had obstructed my view when I was trying to peek in from the outside. I saw two big blue floor mats pushed together side by side on the ground and off in the corner I saw this big stereo boom box. I had no idea what was going on, but I was intrigued and didn't want to leave until I saw what they were doing.

I saw Michael by the boom box and his two older brothers on the mats, and then I saw one of the older brothers move his head in and up and down motion, letting Michael know 'It's time'. When Michael's older brother gave him the nod Michael started the boom box playing. I then saw the weirdest thing I had ever seen in my life. Michael's older brothers were dancing, but they weren't doing any traditional dances that I had ever seen. The two brothers were dancing on every conceivable part of their body, on the tops of their heads, on their knees, on their backs...it was so cool to me. This style of dancing was called 'break dancing' they told me, and they asked if I wanted to try it...I foolishly did. I found out just exactly why they called it what they called it because I felt like I almost broke my whole body trying to do just one of those moves.

I did, however, find one particular move, the knee spin, which was pretty safe and I felt I could do without the fear of breaking anything, so that's what I stuck with. I did that knee spin move everywhere I went, in that basement, in my room, on the sidewalk...I was just nuts about that move because it was something that I felt I could do really well and that's why it stuck with me for quite a long time, but as with anything, it was just a phase and I grew out of it.

I was outside of my apartment one day just walking around when Michael Maldonado came up to me and asked if I would like to go down to his basement, I said of course I would. With just him and I down there maybe I could do my little knee spins, which didn't seem to impress his brothers very much, but maybe they would impress him...he didn't lead me down there to break dance.

He and I went into his apartment complex and then down the stairs to his basement. We didn't go deep into the basement which was were the mats and the boom box were, we just got to the very bottom step and then we suddenly stopped. Michael asked me to lie down on the ground face up, which I did without much hesitation. Michael then asked me to pull my pants down, and that's when I hesitated a little bit. I asked him why he wanted me to pull my pants down, and he said it was because he wanted to suck my dick. There was some discussion about this when he told me what he wanted to do because although I wasn't opposed to him doing that to me, I had been there and done that...which he didn't know, I really wanted to do that to him.

Up to this point I really hadn't thought of him in that certain way before, yeah I thought he was ok looking, but I don't know if I was at the stage where I wanted to perform those kind of acts with him. All of a sudden my whole mindset changed and I was back, in my mind, being what I was before and doing what I was before. I stopped arguing with him about wanting to do it to him and I just quietly pulled my pants down and let him suck me until he was through.

I knew the very next day that I wanted to go back to his house and continue with this situation and perhaps get going what I'd been doing in 1980 in Texas. I never got the chance to get something like that going because the very next day that I went over to his house I stood there in front of the complex, where you had full view of everyone's balcony, and saw his mom there. I asked where Michael was and she told me that Michael was inside and his head was hurting...something to that effect anyway. I found out later on what had happened because one day I saw Michael coming out of his house with a great big bandage on his head. Some kids, for some reason or another I never found out, decided to throw a brick at him and they busted his head wide open. I didn't see Michael Maldonado after that because very soon thereafter they decided to renovate our apartment buildings and we all had to move.

CHAPTER 4:

MEETING THE DEVIL, THE SECOND TIME

After we moved from the stairwell apartments in Germany we got moved by the military into houses, that is where I met Mandy Fredell. Mandy was a cute little blond-haired, blue-eyed girl whom you just knew was trouble because she had an angelic but at the same time wicked smile. Mandy and I became so-so friends and I would always show up at her house because she and I loved to play backgammon together.

I got into playing backgammon because of my sister, who was real good at it, and she taught me how to play. My sister would go over to Mandy's house and play backgammon with her mother, and Mandy and I would follow suit and play backgammon with each other.

Her mom and dad were both heavy smokers and her dad was a drinker, I can't remember if her mom was or not, so I think my sister basically went over there to be a release for Mandy's mom because I believe times were always tense at that house.

I got in very bad trouble over what Mandy and I did one day. I went over to Mandy's house and she asked me if I wanted to go to the park, that's what we called it, but it was just really this big open field with humongous blades of grass, so I said sure. Mandy was so cool-looking that day because she had on blue jeans and a blue jean jacket…those were so popular back then. We went to the park and that's where she pulled them out. She had swiped a couple of her mom's cigarettes and she also had this little baggie with her full of toothpaste.

We stood there for a while talking about it and then we lit up. It didn't take very long to smoke them, but we felt very grown-up. I can remember trying to act so cool, holding it between my pointer finger and my middle finger and pretending I was somebody important...for that few minutes I was smoking anyway. We got done smoking our one cigarette each, dipped our fingers into the bag and rubbed the toothpaste all over our teeth and on our tongues.

When we went home to our respective houses that night I was feeling so excited about having smoked that I let it slip out and I told my brother about it...big mistake. My brother told on me to my parents and I got grounded for it, and I think I was even told to stay away from Mandy...ah, well life goes on.

We lived in a cul-de-sac, and at one end lived a Japanese family. I don't recall the mother's or the father's name, I told you I'm not good with names, but they had two sons named Shozo and Shoji. The eldest son Shozo couldn't have been more than five or six and he was so cute, I mean he was cute in the way that you just wanted to pinch his cheeks or something, and the smaller one was that much cuter. I would go over to their house all the time and would just love being in the mother's company and being with her kids...it was so much fun, even though she hardly spoke a word of English...but she deserved an A for effort.

I would go to this lady's house around the same time every day because every day without fail at this certain time she would always have coffee, and she wouldn't only give me some, but she also gave her kids coffee. I don't know if giving coffee to kids is a Japanese custom or not, but in my house it was forbidden to even go near the stuff unless you were an adult. She kind of, without saying so, put me a little bit in charge of her kids…and I loved it because I would play with these kids and teach them certain things.

There was one day, around Christmas time, when I went over to their house and Shozo was so excited because he had got a brand-new big wheel for Christmas that he wanted to ride right away. I looked at his mom as if to say 'may I?' and she kind of nodded her head. I told Shozo to get on, I grabbed the back of that big wheel and I pushed as hard as I could around and around our street; I could hear him having so much fun and yelling and screaming and screeching with delight…I was in heaven.

This other boy moved in not too long after that and began showing up at their house at about the same time I would. This other little boy would sit down and have discussions with the mother and the kids just like I would. The other little boy would also play with the children just like I would...I was getting pissed off. I was very jealous of him because he came in and it seemed like he was taking over the job that I wanted and was supposed to have. I don't recall whatever happened to that family or the other little kid, but I just know that during that point in time I really hated that kid for taking what was supposed to have been mine.

There was this woman who lived two houses away from us and she provided another moment for me that I will never forget. This lady wasn't married, I think, because I swear I never saw her husband, but she mentioned that she was married. She was a very cool lady and not at all what I thought a typical 'go to work' type of lady was…she had a motorcycle.

My brother and I would always go outside and talk to her, she was a very fun lady to talk to and if we weren't so young at the time, she could have probably told us some stories.

My brother and I went over to her house one day when we saw her pulling into her driveway and we started talking to her. My brother was always the more outgoing one of us so I guess that is why she asked him first if he wanted to go for a ride on her motorcycle; he definitely wanted to do that so of course he said yes. She got in front as he hoped on the back, they both put on their helmets and he had his arms wrapped around her waist so off they went.

They came back from their motorcycle ride about a couple of minutes later, they had gone around the block out of sight, and he was so excited. My brother said, "Man, that was so cool, you should try it."

The lady asked me if I wanted to get on and at first I was very adamant that I did NOT want to get on that motorcycle. My brother, however, kept prodding me and prodding me to do it and the lady kept telling me how safe it was so I relented started getting ready to go for a ride with her on her motorcycle...for me the fun stopped as soon as it started. I got on the back of that bike with her and I put my arms around her waist; I had the tightest grip I have ever had on anybody, she told me to loosen up, but I just couldn't. I saw her legs going from the ground up towards the bike and I felt myself losing my grip on her waist and that's all I needed; I was done with this ride. They tried to convince me to get back on the bike, that everything was going to be fine and that it was perfectly safe, but this little boy was having absolutely NONE of that...I never even went close to that bike ever again.

My old T-ball coach, Gary Lloyd, and his wife and two children,

Christopher and Chelsea, who were living in the same apartment building that we were living in, also had to move, as well as Eric Stemerling and his family. They moved into what I deemed as way better accommodations than we moved in to. Their places were so huge that is was easy to get lost in their houses. I was so lost in their house at one point that I actually banged on the wall until someone came and got me, after that I wasn't allowed to go anywhere unless I had an escort.

When I was in, I believe it was the last year of middle school that I spent in Germany I met an English teacher that forever changed my life. I can't for the life of me remember that teacher's name (as usual), but I will never forget his face or what he did for me. This English teacher, to me, looked EXACTLY like Gene Wilder in *Willy Wonka And The Chocolate Factory* and the funny thing about that was that *Charlie And The Chocolate Factory* happened to be one of the books we had to read in his class. He read that book out loud and it seemed to come alive for me, and from that day forward I've always loved to read...not when forced but only for fun. That English teacher also loved Roald Dahl books and his favorite was *The Twits*. He used to read *The Twits* all the time in class whenever he could and I grew to love it to, someday I'll buy a copy.

We had a cat when we were living in Germany and I don't remember what his/her name was, but I do remember that we had that cat in the basement most times, and sometimes when we would come home from school my mom would have all these scratches on her from the cat.

One day she decided that the cat had to go, but my brother said that if the cat went then he would go. My sister and I waited for him to go out of the house and then we snuck that cat down to an animal shelter...I wonder if it's too late to trade the cat for my brother.

At this point in my life I had moved from Texas in 1980 to Germany in 1983 and now I was in England and it was 1986. I'd had an interesting and eventful life so far as you can tell, but my 'growing up' so to speak was actually done in England. In England I learned far more than any pre-adolescent should know, and by the time I left England I had done way more than any adolescent should ever have done.

When we arrived in England we stayed in a TLF (temporary living facility) before moving onto base housing. My brother and I used to get picked up from the TLF and bussed to school every day. We weren't in that TLF for long before my brother started making trouble.

We were coming home from school one day on the bus and my brother picked a fight with this other boy. The bus driver had enough of them talking trash back and forth to one another and told them to get off. As I was still too young at the time and didn't know my way around very well, I was forced to get off as well...let me tell you if I did know my way around there would have been no way I was going to get off that bus.

My brother, the other boy, and I got off the bus together as well as a whole bunch of other kids...you know the mentality, everyone wanting to see a fight. As soon as we got off the bus and there was that circle of kids around us, my brother and this kid started fighting and the kid gave my brother a bloody nose. My brother tried to make excuses for it and even brought me into the act by saying, "Go ahead, Brad, tell him how easy it is to get my nose to bleed." I guess he said this hoping that would tell the other boy that maybe his nose wasn't tough, but the rest of him was…I didn't even say a word. My brother and I had walked home from where the bus dropped us off that night and he swore me to secrecy. I said that I would never tell anyone about that fight…and I haven't, until now.

While in England we got to visit a really nice place called Somerset. My distant cousins, or something like that, were there and that was the reason we went to Somerset. We got out of the car to meet our British relatives and they all remarked that our station wagon looked like a bus, in England it seems they all have small cars.

We spent about a week there I think, and all I can remember is drinking lots of tea and playing lots of darts. They not only liked, but they LOVED their tea in England. They had their teatime promptly at five o'clock every afternoon and I drank with the mom of the household every day because she was sweet and I liked her. After a while I was getting very sick of having tea all the time...but I still drank it.

That family had a boy who was about my brother's age and we all had a good time playing darts together every day; I even got kind of good at it. I hated that sometimes, because they were practically the same age, the boy and my brother would gang up on me and tease me mercilessly…I guess that's the price little brother's pay though so I just had to take it.

I liked Somerset, and I am sad that I'll probably never get to go back, but those were some fun and fond memories for me.

When I arrived at my new middle school, my parents, and the faculty I guess, thought it would be best to put me in special education, which I thought was so weird because I didn't think I had any special needs, I just thought I had poor eyesight. There were no special education classes that a person could take, but for one period a day you would go to a classroom and there were people in there that were geared towards helping people with special needs. Ms. Riley was the main special education teacher in that classroom and she had a helper by the name of Mr. Brown.

We all would usually go in there about three times a day…once at the start of the day to get a little card so you could pass around to all your teachers and they could mark down whether you were a good student or a bad student. You went there again when it was your hour to go and benefit from the special education class, and once at the end of the day so you could turn in your little sheet and you could go home. EVERY time that you entered that room the rule was that you had to take your shoes off, this I thought was a very dumb rule.

I met a couple of people through being in that special education class named Kevin Price and David Noreiga, who actually ended up coming to my house on one occasion that was very weird, which I will explain later. In Ms. Riley's class is also where I met my very best friend, which I'll also tell you about a little later.

That place to me was more like a second-grade classroom than a place where just outside those doors was a middle school where people actually acted normally. In this room you had the no shoes rule, you had the 'let me check your slip so I can see if you were good' rule, and you even had strange consequences if you were bad.

On the little slip they gave you to take to your teachers they would count up all the 'O's' for outstanding. Then later they would go out and buy things at a store and have a little sale where you could buy things. The better you were at getting 'outstanding', the more you would get to choose from...it was like an old-fashioned *The Price Is Right*. I went along with it because I couldn't honestly do anything else, but I thought it was very stupid.

The consequences for doing badly in that particular class were something out of the dark ages. If you cursed or talked back to them, they would give you a little warning. However, if you persisted, they would come over to where you were sitting, pinch your nose shut and hold their other hand over your mouth, thereby cutting off your air circulation for about five to ten seconds. The first time I saw this hold being put into effect I got very scared for myself. I lightened up the second time I saw it because when Mr. Brown was putting his hand over one boy's mouth, the boy bit him. I couldn't help but laugh when the boy bit Mr. Brown, but I didn't laugh too hard for fear they would come after me.

I had a friend named Robert Kassin, I don't really know why he was my friend because sometimes he could be kind of a jerk, and then again sometimes he was cool, so I let it slide.

One day I was in the bowling alley doing my bowling tournament thing and it wasn't my turn so I went in to the games room to play a little pinball when Robert came up to me looking very mad. Robert said something to the effect that my brother was supposed to come over and baby-sit his little sister, but that he had come over to the house, scared her and started waving a knife around. He started making all these unfounded accusations towards my brother and I was asking myself, 'Why is he bringing this to my attention instead of telling someone in authority?' That's when he jumped on me in the games room. I have to tell you I'm not a fighter, but I did angrily push him away and then when we were outside the games room we had a very heated argument, but luckily someone was there to break it up. I don't know why Robert said these things and I will never know if any of them were true, but I do hate the fact that I was forced into fighting for my brother because that isn't something that I ever wanted to do.

On one particular night when my mom and dad were out of the house my brother gave me a memory I won't be forgetting any time soon. The incident with my brother seemed to be over just as quickly as it happened and I don't remember what caused the situation and, likewise, I don't remember how it ended, but I do have a vivid picture in my mind of what happened that night.

My mom and dad went out and I guess I must have been sitting on the couch. I don't remember where my sister had been, but all of a sudden there she was, standing in front of me right next to our telephone and my brother not five steps in front of her holding a knife and threatening something. When my sister reached for the phone, my brother took the knife and slashed right through the phone cord. I must have blocked the rest of it out because I can't remember any more about that night.

My brother at this point in time was into alcohol, I don't know if he was into drugs as well then, but I suspect that he was. I heard stories about him trying to come through windows to get back into the house and falling, and just random crazy things like that which I sort of refused to believe until I witnessed it for myself. There were a lot of days when I can recall my family being called to go look for him somewhere or to go pick him up because he was drunk and causing all sorts of problems. A twelve-year-old boy enjoys a lot of things but going with his mom and dad in the family station wagon to look for his drunken brother is not one of those things.

I remember the night I first felt my brother's touch like it was yesterday. My sister had gone out for the night, who knows where, and my parents were getting ready to go out as well, which was fine with me because I was watching TV.

My parents shut the door behind them and I'd been watching TV for about twenty minutes or so when the unexpected happened. I heard the footsteps of my brother coming downstairs while I continued to watch TV. The TV, as I was watching it, all of a sudden turned off and I saw this figure moving from beside me to the front of me. I looked up and I saw my brother standing right in front of me totally naked. I looked up at him as if to ask him what he wanted and all he said was, "Suck me."

I'd seen the way my brother had acted before so of course I did what he said to do without any question. I didn't know what would happen if I didn't do it, and to be honest, even though this was the first time my brother had approached me like this, I was, by now, a robot in sexual matters. I was doing anything and everything anybody told me to do so it wasn't like I made a conscious choice to do it, but he just said to do it and I did it. I don't remember feeling anything while I was doing it or after I did it. I didn't feel any emotion whatsoever; no pain or anger or embarrassment or anything like that because to me that kind of stuff was normal so I really didn't think anything about it at the time.

This kind of attention from my brother went on for a very long time, approximately eight years and almost daily. For a long while it was the same old thing, where my brother would get naked and instruct me what to do and I just did it like I was some kind of sex robot or something, but after a while he started getting more inventive.

I will never forget one particular day when everyone was out of the house. My brother came towards me and I instinctively started taking off my clothes, he said, "Hold on, we're gonna try something different today." My brother led me from his room downstairs to my parent's room where he started going through my mom's underwear drawer. My brother pulled out one of my mom's stockings and told me to put it on, which I did, and then he went into the drawer again and pulled out one of my mom's bra's and instructed me to put that on as well, which I also did. I'm actually glad that I was robotic in my sexual thinking back then because if I weren't, I would have probably found some way to mess myself up and I would be a different person than who I turned out to be today.

My brother wasn't done with his sexual perversions with me because one day he came into my room and asked me to follow him to his room, which I did, and he took out what looked like some little pieces of rope. He told me to lie face up on the bed and told he was going to tie me to it.

I never actually said no to any of the things that he told me to do. I don't know if I was just set in my way of thinking and just didn't mind it, or if I just didn't care anymore, or perhaps I was so afraid of him that I just did what he wanted for fear of what he would do if I didn't.

I was lying on the bed as he instructed me, and he told me to spread my arms and legs out in a spread-eagle position. My brother took one of those small pieces of rope and I could feel him tying my right foot to the bed, and he told me this was going to be fun. I can only remember the first thing he said to me, but every time he tied an arm or a leg to the bed he would say something to me. There I was tied to the bed and I remember thinking to myself that this could be very interesting, and I was even a little turned on by it. My brother started out kind of tickling me and then before I knew it his hands and mouth were everywhere on me. The situations that we were in never lasted very long, sometimes only like ten minutes and then we would go back to doing our normal everyday routine as if nothing were any different.

It was a very strange time for me because I had all these emotions welling up inside of me like, why did my brother pick me? I like doing things with him, sometimes I would just like it if he left me alone. All these feelings were welling up inside of me at the same time so I couldn't really make sense of them, and I didn't even try…I just did what I was told when I was told.

I had some measure of control over my brother one night that I play back often in my mind. The night started off like any other night, with my sister nowhere around, she was probably hanging out with her friends, my mom and dad going out for some reason or another, and my brother left home alone with me. My brother started in with our same routine, him being naked right in front of me and I was instructed to suck him off. After so many minutes of me sucking him off, that's when he told me to take my clothes off. Up until this time my brother had always been just content with sucking each other, and maybe once in a while he had me fuck him...and when I say once in a while, I just mean not daily, but this time he had something else in mind. My brother told me to lay down on the floor with my butt up in the air. I turned my head and I saw my brother grabbing the Vaseline jar; I knew what he wanted to do. I let my brother go about one inch inside of me with his penis and then I screamed REAL LOUD. I immediately told him to take it out and to never try and fuck me ever again, and then I promptly went upstairs and shit blood.

To tell the truth, I really don't know whether the fact that I was able to dictate to him what I wanted to do, in that situation, makes me kind of a slut or not because maybe he WOULD have listened to me had I opened up my mouth and told him I really didn't want to do this. But of course by this point in time I really couldn't have told you whether I did or I didn't want to do this.

There was one particular day when I thought everything that my brother was doing to me was going to end...no such luck.

My brother and I were home alone again, and he decided that it might be nice for us to take a shower together. I thought that this was pretty ok, at least it was better than jumping into the sex stuff right away...I don't know what I was thinking, my head was pretty messed up by this time. My brother instructed me to take my clothes off and get in the shower, which I did with no complaining whatsoever. He then turned on the water, took HIS clothes off, and jumped in the shower with me. We stood there kissing and caressing like two people that were in love or something, I look back with mixed emotions about that particular event. After we had been kissing and caressing for a while I just instinctively went down to his crotch area and started pleasing him like I knew only I could...we didn't even hear the car door shut.

My parents had come back from wherever they had gone and they were on their way upstairs. My brother and I were oblivious to the noise that was going on outside that closed bathroom door so we didn't even hear when my dad's hand was turning the bathroom doorknob. My dad opened the bathroom door (we were still oblivious to this because the shower curtain blocked our view and we were too wrapped up in what we were doing to see what was about to happen), and he was treated to the shock of his life.

There I was, naked and standing with my equally naked brother in the shower for all to see, and my dad said, "What are you two doing?"

I thought it was great that he had caught us because finally he was going to know everything that was going on between my brother and I, and he would be powerful enough to stop it from ever happening again...how wrong I was.

I don't remember having a big discussion about this event with my parents, and I know my brother didn't say much because something definitely would have happened if he had said something. I was angry with my dad for not stopping him, but how could he have known? I was angry with him for not pressing one of us into telling him what was going on so that he COULD stop it. I don't know whether it was embarrassment or because that's what I thought love was that prevented me from finally telling my parents what was going on between us, but I never did tell them what had happened that day or what was continuing to go on every time that they left the house; I kept that secret locked deep inside me.

My mom and dad apparently had a fight with my brother because one day I turned around and he was living with the next-door neighbor. I don't really know what happened between my parents and my brother, and I'm not going to ask, but one day he was living in our house and the next minute he wasn't. I missed my brother during those times because I knew that if he was living next door then we wouldn't be able to continue what we were doing, and I missed that.

I also was afraid for the next-door neighbors because they had a little boy who couldn't have been more than six or seven at the time and I just had a feeling that my brother and their son were going to do something together, and for some reason that made me very jealous of the boy. I liked that boy, don't get me wrong, because he was sweet and kind and when I saw him riding his big wheel I would always say hi, or if he was outside playing I would make a point of going up and talking to him and sometimes playing with him. But when my brother went to live over there with that family, I became very jealous of him because I could actually picture him and my brother in my mind doing things that my brother only used to do with me.

I had a friend in middle school named Sarah. Sarah was a very tall girl with pretty, wavy, blond hair and she must have lived in our neighborhood because it seemed to me like she was always around, yet I never knew where she lived.

One day I was wandering around outside and she came up to me and started talking to me. She asked me if I wanted to play this game called Kirby. I said sure I would play Kirby with her, and I asked her how you played it. She said that you take a ball and both stand on opposite sides of the street with your feet next to the curb. Then you throw the ball towards the curb, trying to get it to bounce off the curb and then you would run up and try to catch it, and if you did catch it, then you won. There was a whole points system to this game and it was very easy to play, especially since we lived in a cul-de-sac so hardly any cars were coming in and out. Sarah and I would play that game for hours. We would just stand out there and play and talk and have a good old time. I found out much later, and quite by accident by going to the backyard and finding them, that Sarah and my brother were boyfriend and girlfriend. The fact that Sarah was my brother's girlfriend pissed me off a whole lot because Sarah was supposed to be

MY friend, NOT his.

There were so many times when I wanted to ruin it for my brother and tell Sarah everything about what had been happening between him and me, not that I thought what we were doing was wrong, but just because I wanted to break them up.

In my last year of middle school in England I got something that I didn't ever want to get...my brother's old teacher. The teacher's name was Mrs. Mitchell, and to me she was a scary looking lady. My brother had caused so much trouble in her class that when I was there I didn't tell her I was his younger brother. She was a smart cookie though and she figured out I WAS his younger brother, and she kept her eye on me the entire time I was in her class...that's one class I'm glad I'm out of now.

There was a lady named Tammy who lived right across the street from us. Tammy was a certified home caregiver to children; in other words seven or eight kids would be dropped off at Tammy's house and then picked up once their moms and dads came home from work. I loved going over there because not only would I get to talk to Tammy, who I liked very much because she was easy to talk to, but it meant I would also be able to play with all the kids. I'm a big kid at heart and enjoy being around them, so if I get a chance to be around a child, then you bet I'm going to be there.

My mom liked going over to Tammy's as well, I guess it was like my mom's getaway from dealing with all three of us kids. And she loved to be around the kids as well...the small ones I mean.

One day at Tammy's house, my mom and Tammy were both outside talking and watching some of the other older kids play, and I was inside with two or three kids that were at the table eating. I don't know where I got this idea from, but I saw this boy in overalls sitting at the table and just quietly eating his lunch. The boy couldn't have been that old because although he was in a chair, he was also in a booster seat. I walked up to him, slipped one of his overall straps to one side exposing his nipple, and I put my mouth on it. To this very day I don't know why I put my mouth on his nipple, but for some reason I didn't feel disgusted at the time for doing so.

The night my brother was taken away from me is a night filled with mixed emotions for me. The day started just like any other day, I had gone to work at the childcare center, just like I had done every day that summer. When I got out of work I took that little short walk I have always taken from the childcare center to the bowling alley to get ready for my league game. My mom and dad and sister were all there cheering me on in my bowling match, I felt so much love that night that the way the night ended I felt kind of cheated.

We all piled in the car and drove home afterwards. I got out of the car, I'm always out of the car first because I have my hand on the door handle even before the car stops, and went straight for the front door. When I got there I found a note taped on the door and it was signed by my brother. It said that if we went in there he was going to kill us, but it specifically asked for my parents to go in the house so that he could kill them.

I was the first one to read the note and you would think that since I was only twelve or thirteen at the time I would have been terrified about reading that, but all I remember is being full of anger and wanting to go inside and rip him apart.

I never got the chance to rip him apart because at that point my parents got to the door, read the note and told my sister to take me across the street to Tammy's house.

When got inside of Tammy's house, she and her husband were as comforting as they could be, and we waited there for what seemed to me like a very long time. Finally, I just couldn't take it anymore and I went outside and stood at the top of the hill where her house was to watch the drama unfold.

I really couldn't see much of what was going on, but I saw an ambulance in our driveway and it seemed to be there for a very long time; I was very terrified by this. I could see a bike racing my way, but I couldn't see who was on it until it was right beside me. I saw then that it was only one of the neighborhood kids, but as it was coming up to me I got this feeling in my stomach that my brother had gotten away and was coming to kill me.

That night was the longest night I ever spent in England, and I was glad it was over when I saw the ambulance drive away.

My parents came over, thanked Tammy and her husband and asked if we wanted to come sleep in our house or if we just wanted to sleep there that night. I opted to sleep in our own house because there was no way in hell I was going to let my brother terrify me out of sleeping in my own house...I do, however, remember being scared the entire night and not getting much sleep at all.

When my brother left it was like the whole bottom had dropped out and I was left with nowhere to go. My brother had been a central part of my life for so long, because of the fact that he told me what to do and when to do it, that I was totally lost and didn't know what I was going to do next...the result wasn't pretty.

CHAPTER 5:

AFTERMATH

I became hyper hormonal as a result of my brother leaving, which meant I thought about doing something with someone all day every day.

I would go to school and see all these boys and I would wonder what they looked like naked, or I would wonder if they would mind if I sucked them off. I would have dreams almost nightly of having my way with one of those boys or I would dream about them dominating me, this went on all the time until we got back to the states and I was reunited with my brother...even though he was in drug rehab and couldn't get out.

One day a family came over to visit us and they had a little girl who couldn't have been more than four or five at the time. I led this girl, who trusted me, up to my room and let her play on the floor. I got up on my bed, pulled my pants down and started jacking off. She looked at me as if to say 'what are you doing?' and I kind of coached her to touch it. I didn't have any remorse at the time about what I made that little girl do.

I had many friends in England, and I don't use that term loosely at all. One of my best friends in the whole world was a boy named Michael Freeman. Michael Freeman and I did a lot of things together...to my surprise none of those things were sexual. I have to say right here and now that probably the reason he was my very best friend is the fact that he and I didn't look at each other in a sexual way, at least I didn't...at first.

Michael and I were in class one day and we had a very heated discussion, a nose-to-nose kind of discussion, and this girl walked by us and said, "You two look like you wanna kiss." I was very embarrassed by the kissing comment she had made for two reasons. One was the fact that I was just starting basically to get into puberty and I kind of looked to this girl and thought she was very pretty, and that maybe I could get something going with her. The second reason I was embarrassed was the fact that, for a split second, I kind of enjoyed being that close to him and my mind wandered and wondered what would happen if… My mind only wandered that way for a split second though, and it was over before anything could really happen.

We were in science class when this whole mess about the 'kiss' started. I loved science class because we got to dissect things, put things into beakers and blow stuff up; it was all just real cool to me. Michael Freeman and I would always sit together at the front of the class.

There is a certain stigma attached to people who sit in the front of the class that they are the nerds of the class, I don't really think we were nerds. The front of the class is just were we ended up and it seemed like a fun place to stay because it was by the teacher and he was cool to us. He was the only teacher I can recall that ever let us bring drinks into the classroom. When I say drinks I don't really mean he let us bring any kind of drink we wanted into the class, we brought in our mugs and he would fill them. I had this bright red mug that I would bring in almost every day that I was in his class, and he would take it and fill it with hot cocoa. I can't for the life of me remember his name, I suck at remembering names as you already know, but I will never forget his face. This man had to be in his late forties, early fifties because he had a little bit of a receding hairline and although he had a full head of hair it was very salt and peppery in the middle and the sides were totally gray. I will never forget his class and his way of teaching it, he would just basically let you do what you wanted to in his class in the context of the lesson that was being taught that day…I felt so free and independent for one of the first times in my life.

Band was a fun class for me. My teacher's name was Mr. Skiles (one I do remember), and he was the friendliest teacher you would ever want to meet. We had to pick what instrument we wanted to play that year and the instrument I would be playing was the clarinet. I actually got stuck with the clarinet because my sister had an old clarinet and it was better than having to fork out more dough for another instrument.

Actually when I look back on it now, the clarinet was a good choice for me just for the fact that it had been my sister's because it was like a family tradition thing…even though only two kids out of the three played instruments.

One day we actually had a big musical production in front of the whole high school auditorium…hey it wasn't Carnegie Hall, but it was something. I was so nervous playing my little clarinet in that big band, not because I had stage fright or anything like that, but because I was just hoping I wasn't going to screw up...I didn't.

I actually went into Ms. Riley's class one day with my clarinet case. Mr. Brown saw me with it, came over and said to me "You're a regular Benny Goodman, aren't you?" I just stared at him like he was from another planet, but then he told me Benny Goodman was a clarinet player so I was like 'yeah I am' even though I still had absolutely no clue who the man was.

Ms. Riley had an adopted son named Jason. Jason was an Asian looking guy of about twenty or so and looked like that Asian guy in *Karate Kid part 2*.

One day I was out on the blacktop just walking around, the blacktop was HUGE. It had chalk marks all over it for hopscotch games, and it had squares drawn in chalk. These squares were drawn into four smaller squares and a person would stand in each one. Then they would toss a ball into another person's square and you couldn't let the ball bounce twice otherwise you were out of the game...it's strange the things we did for fun back then. In the far middle left of the blacktop was a basketball hoop where three or four guys were playing basketball and having a good time. The basketball got stuck in the trees up above the hoop so Jason came out to get the ball down. Trying to think of something to get the ball down with he took a brush, put it on the end of a jump rope and kept swinging at the ball so he could kind of lasso the ball until it came down.

I wasn't aware that this was going on and I walked right in the middle of what they were doing. I heard them kind of shouting, but I just thought they were having fun...little did I know why they were shouting at me. Jason knew I had poor eyesight and he was trying to yell at me to get out of the way, but that brush came swooping down at me at a very fast and hard velocity, hitting me right in the left upper cheek. The brush that hit me wasn't a soft brush, but one with a wooden handle and thick wire bristles, but I didn't cry once.

Blood started pouring out of my mouth so fast that by the time I got to the nurses' office the entire front of my shirt was soaked in it. I remember the school nurse telling me I looked like I had just been through World War II...she looked old enough to remember that.

I was in a bowling league when I was in England. I wasn't a very good player, but I loved playing the game. I loved the tournament style of it just because that when it wasn't your turn to bowl you had time to go off and eat some fries or play some video games or things like that…my favorite game of all time has to be pinball because you don't really have to use your brain to play it.

There was this really serious bowler named Jason Merribaugh who was decked out in professional bowling gear. Jason had the whole collection of bowling shoes, his own bowling ball, and a rosin bag so his hands didn't get to sticky…he was a SERIOUS bowler. Jason was a great bowler as well because he was always in the top ten or higher.

My bowling skills left a little something to be desired, I was as far down as you could go and gave new meaning to the words 'you stink'. The one thing that validated my place in bowling history was the fact that we played in this national tournament and I actually won a spot in that tournament, ok so it was the very bottom spot, but I still got there. I remember feeling so sad for the kid I beat for that spot because it wasn't like I beat him by a lot, I only beat him by one pin…kind of pathetic when you think about two boys fighting to hold on to last place. The boy and I did our little handshake at the end of the bowling match, but after that I could see him in the corner crying…I just wanted to die. When I won the bottom spot in the tournament we actually got to go on a ferryboat and go to another country to compete with other people…we went to Germany.

I was thinking to myself, *I was just there a couple of years ago and now I have to go back*, but the whole experience was fun and I got to do something that I'd never done before. We got to take a ferry to Germany and my dad went with me, because I could take one parent along, and while he spent most of his time sleeping in the upstairs part of the ferry I was downstairs learning a new hobby. I was twelve when I took that trip to Germany on that ferry and I had no way of knowing what I was doing was illegal.

My friends and I that were on the ferry went down to the games room that they had there. My dad had given me some money so I was going to go down and play a few video games when I saw this game with a big large handle on the side that looked like a joystick so I put my British pound in the machine and pulled the lever. You can imagine my surprise when down at the bottom there were nine more of those shiny British pounds.

Someone told me that what I was doing was wrong and that it was called gambling, so I toyed with the idea a little bit of telling my dad because I didn't want to get into trouble for it, even though I didn't know what I was doing was bad. I finally told my dad and he took my British pounds away from me...that'll teach me to keep my big mouth shut.

The bowling tournament was ok, nothing really special, but because I slept in the room with others I did get to see some boys in their underwear...yeah I was still thinking about that very heavily, even thought I didn't want those feelings and I didn't know why I was having them. The bowling tournament was over, we hopped on that ferry back to England and I resumed my life just as if I had never left...I didn't even place anywhere in that tournament.

We got back to England and my best friend Mike Freeman was having a birthday so he asked me if I wanted to come over, and I said sure. Michael also asked me if I wanted to sleep over, and I agreed.

There were about three or four other boys there and all I could remember thinking is that I wanted to get something sexual going with them.

It was time for bed and I got more aroused because some of them slept in their underwear so I would come up to them (I still can't tell you why I did it) with like a blanket on my head and sort of feel around like I didn't have any idea where I was going. I managed to touch a few boys in the crotch, if Michael found out what I was really doing he probably would have kicked me out.

I had gotten to ride the bus home from school a few times and on one of these occasions I met this bus driver that sort of changed my life for the better.

These bus drivers were all British and I totally loved their accent; especially this one bus driver that I befriended because his accent to me was the best.

I got on the bus one day and for some reason that was the day I recognized his eyes. I asked him about him having dark circles under his eyes and if he tired. I then suggested that he should get some sleep or something. He told me that the bags weren't because he was tired; they were because he had been robbed and they had cut him multiple times. After hearing that this robbery had happened to him and how he had been cut up by these people, I had a better sense of right and wrong and I never forgot that bus driver's story, and I never will.

I only went on the bus a few times; after that for some reason they thought I should be driven to school in a taxi. For some reason I had labeled it the 'bad boy' taxi. I labeled it that because I thought only bad people got told to ride in it, but then there was this other girl that used to ride in it with us, and, although I never asked, I didn't think she could have done anything bad so there went my 'bad boy' taxi theory.

This taxi idea was put together by Ms. Riley, whom at this point in time I loved very much because she was always very sweet to me.

On one particular day my whole attitude towards Ms. Riley changed and it never recovered. I was up in my room reading or something and there was a knock at my door. I was told some friends were here to see me. I went downstairs and David Noriega and Kevin Price were down there waiting for me. I asked what they wanted and they said they needed to talk to me urgently so we went up to my room to talk.

When we got up to my room David was talking to me about his dad being very bad to him and that he wanted me to take a look at something. He then pulled down his pants a little bit to show me a big red welt. Of course I was very concerned for him at this moment, but sadly one of the things going through my mind at that particular moment was that I wished Kevin had pulled HIS pants down.

We all went downstairs to tell my mother this information, Kevin left and then the phone rang. My mom picked up the phone and it was Ms. Riley. She stated that she wanted to talk to David and that was when the whole mood of the house got really weird.

Ms. Riley was talking to David and all of a sudden David started crying on the phone. My mom abruptly took the phone from David and started talking to Ms. Riley, and then my mom started crying. First of all I wondered what this woman could be saying to make my mom cry and I begged my mom to hand me the phone; I was almost going to rip it out of her hands when she hung up.

I spent quite a few minutes consoling both David and my mother and after having to do that I was VERY pissed at Mr. Riley.

I went into school the next day with the express purpose of giving Ms. Riley a piece of my mind for making my mother cry. I confronted her about it, but she explained it away with some cheap-ass answer, but things were never the same between us again...I felt sorry now that one year I had actually asked her to come to my parents wedding anniversary party.

I was riding in the taxi with the girl and this classmate of mine named Chris Pavlas. I liked the girl that rode with us because she was always so sweet and kind to me, but when she got out of the car it was a different story. Chris Pavlas was always a jerk to me. Chris would call me names and do things to me that were very demeaning, I had a large forehead because of all the scar tissue that was in there and he took full advantage of it several time by actually calling me a dickhead, stating that my head looked like that. I hated Chris with a passion, but mostly I hated him for comments like that.

That's also why I kind of disliked my mom this one day. Because our taxi was running late, or had broken down or something like that, my mom picked Chris and I up from the school and she even dropped him off at his house. I remember thinking that how dare she pick Chris up, my enemy, and drop him off anywhere...didn't she know how cruel he was to me? I realize now that if I had said something back then, things might have gone a little differently, but I was too embarrassed back then to admit that he was teasing and torturing me, let alone the things that he was saying to me.

There was one time when our whole class went to the library to see an exhibit of some kind, and that was one day that I was really terrified for my life. We all went to the library and when we got there the teacher started talking, who really pays attention at times like these anyway. I looked up from where I was and I saw these two boys who had been teasing me off and on that whole year. They sort of looked at me with that 'I'm gonna get you now' look, and proceeded to chase me around the tables that were in there and up and down different aisles until the whole presentation was over. I really felt for my life that day because I didn't know what they would do if they ever caught me and I was very afraid, luckily they never caught me and that was then end of that.

In high school I got blessed with having NO gym classes at all, but that wasn't the case in middle school. Since I was part of a special education class, I was also part of a special education gym class, which I hated. We wouldn't do much in that class, just a couple tucks and rolls and sit-ups and stuff, and maybe play a few games now and then, nothing really strenuous. Even though it wasn't what I would call a 'real' gym class, we still had to suit up like we were in one, and that is the ONLY thing I liked about that class.

Because of where my mind was at that particular point in my life, I definitely enjoyed going into that locker room knowing that I was going to see ten to twenty boys in nothing but their underwear. I thought to myself that I would definitely do anything any of those boys told me to do.

On one particular day I got the chance to do just that. Four or five boys were all in a huddle like formation all around me and they were kind of teasing me a bit because they thought they saw me looking at one of the boys. The boy that I was accused of looking at was wearing nothing at the time but his underwear and he said to me, "You wanna see my dick, don't you?" and with that he pulled down his underwear and said, "Go ahead take a look, you know you want to."

At this point in time I was feeling like I had to save face because if I had looked, they would have jumped all over me and I would have been labeled for the rest of my stay at that middle school. I never did bother looking when that boy pulled down his underwear, but oh God did I want to.

There was a family in England that we had gotten somewhat close to called Moyer. In this family were Don Sr., Don Jr., Toni, Alton, and Crystal. Don Jr. was about my age, maybe a year older, and he was the one that I liked hanging out with. Crystal was so cute because she was real young at the time and couldn't pronounce my name, so whenever I went to their house she would always call me 'Bwadwee'. I got endless teasing from Don Jr. and Alton for this...but it was a good kind of teasing and it was funny. I would tell Alton or Don something and they would say, "Ok, Bwadwee," and I'd just turn around and give them a look like I was ticked at them for saying that, but they knew it was ok...which only made them do it more.

For some unknown reason I would always make Don Jr. muffins before going down to his house. Once a week I made him muffins and I would call him and say, "I'm on my way," and I would walk those muffins all the way down to his house, which wasn't very far, but it was odd that I was doing that. The more I think about it in later years, the more I know now that I really wasn't doing it JUST to bring him muffins...I was there to take a look at Alton.

Alton was a very cute kid to me. I walked to his house one day, went into his room and saw him playing video games with a friend, only Alton was completely shirtless. Alton was a couple of years younger than I was and the image of him sitting on his bed totally shirtless made me stay in his room for quite a while, and I wasn't looking at the game that he and his friend were playing...I was looking right at him. To say that I went back to his house was an understatement; I went back almost ALL the time...so much so that they probably thought I lived there. I went back and I baked Don Jr. muffins all the time and walked them up to his house just for the express purpose of seeing Alton without a shirt again...which I never did.

I was going outside to play one day and was in my yard looking for something to do when this boy Philip, who was nine or ten at the time, came up to me and we started talking. He had blond hair and blue eyes and he was a really cute kid, and that's when it happened.

I went over to the side of my house with this boy and continued to talk with him, we then sat down and carried on talking. I don't know how it came about, but I ended up with his foot in my hand and I was tickling it; I then put it up towards my mouth and licked his foot.

My dad came around the corner at this point and assumed that I was just tickling his foot, which I let him assume, and then he left.

I started talking to Philip about 'getting ready' for what women were going to want to do with him once he got older. I asked him if he wanted to go into my house so I could show him what I meant and he agreed to come in.

We walked up to my room where I locked the door and told him to get on the bed. I grabbed a toy and gave it to him so he would have something to play with because he was apprehensive about what I was doing until I gave him the toy. I pulled his shirt up over his head and just began kissing and licking every inch of his body that I could see, but he started to laugh so I stopped because I didn't want anyone to come upstairs. I was talking to Philip the whole time and telling him that this was what a girl was going to do to him when he got older and I was preparing him for it; he seemed to not mind what I was doing to him.

I told Philip to roll over on his stomach and I pulled down his pants to look at his butt. I spent a few seconds just staring at it and then I took my hands and rubbed them all over before placing my mouth on and inside. I continued to make sure that he knew why I was doing this so it seemed ok with him that this was happening.

I told him to turn over on his back and I found myself staring at his penis. I took his penis in my mouth and played with it for a few minutes, I got up then and tried to put my penis in his mouth, but when he didn't want to do that I told him to get up and get dressed. Then I proceeded to lie there on the bed and pleasure myself.

I heard a knock on the door and my dad asking if there was anything wrong; I told him there wasn't. He tried to open the door and couldn't, and when he asked why he couldn't I told him it must be jammed because I couldn't open it either, that was because I was still on the bed with my pants down. I unlocked the door and opened it.

My dad kind of looked at me and asked in a discrete way if I had done anything, and I said I hadn't. I usually saw Philip all the time on my street talking to different neighbors on my block, but after this particular day I never saw Philip again.

CHAPTER 6:
THE DEVIL'S RETURN

We loaded up the moving van on our last few days in England and we set out for our newest destination, which was Texas. We were supposed to be stationed in Texas next anyway, but we went there a couple of months early because of the stunt that my brother pulled that got him sent to a rehab facility. My mother was very worried that whole trip down to Texas about how my brother was doing in rehab and things like that, I couldn't have cared less.

I loved our big trip that we took from England to Texas because at this point in time I was fourteen and I was enjoying being a teenager and seeing the sights of all the different places, and enjoying being free and out from under my brother's influence.

My mom was worried all the way up until we got to the front door of the drug rehab place. We went in and seated at the front desk was a lady that looked to me like a grown-up Natalie from *The Fact's Of Life*, which I thought was very cool. We asked her to page my brother in the other building. He came down and hugged my mother on October 28, 1989, a few minutes after midnight...right after my brother's birthday.

I had started ninth grade in England for a couple of months and then when we moved to Texas I got to finish out all of my years of high school, which I totally enjoyed because usually we were moving around every three years so I never actually finished going to one school...I just sort of moved on to the next one. Ironically we moved into another cul-de-sac, it seems we were a cul-de-sac family, and we met some nice neighbors while we were there.

We lived right across the street from an elderly couple who looked to be in their sixties or seventies. The woman was British and the man wasn't so although I liked the man I instantly took a liking to the woman because I love British accents.

This couple had a few dogs and that's originally how I got to know them. I was outside one day when she was taking her dogs out for a walk and I went over and started talking to her. Her husband always had the garage door open all the way up, which I thought was dangerous in this day and age because anybody could just walk in, and he was always tinkering around there with his little tools on a motorcycle or an engine or something like that. I would always go over and talk to him when he was outside in his garage.

On one particular fourth of July the woman was standing outside watching the fireworks and I came outside to join her, as well as my mom, and we just stood there looking at the fireworks and talking for hours…how I miss that.

My brother was in that drug rehab place for what seemed to me to be an awfully long time. There were some aspects about going there that I liked, and then there were some that I absolutely hated with a passion. We would always have to go in through the front and meet the girl that looked like Natalie from *The Facts Of Life*, which I totally enjoyed doing because she always had a smile on her face. This girl would call someone from the other building and we would get ushered back to the complex where all the 'inmates' were. It was an ok looking place, but I always had a sense of dread about going there, as if I knew something was going to happen and I knew I wasn't going to like it…which happened on many occasions.

At that rehab clinic was also where we met my brother's counselor and he was a very nice man, too bad he had to deal with my brother.

They had a games room at there and my brother showed it to me and throughout the time I spent visiting him I got really good at playing *Super Mario Brothers*. Eventually we went out and bought a game system and that very game, and now every single time I play it I'm reminded of visiting that drug rehab place where my brother was 'incarcerated'.

There was an aspect of being there which I totally hated and that was the therapy sessions which the whole family had to be involved in. One particular therapy session had my mom and brother giving each other a hug and crying. I just wanted to stand up and walk right out of that room or shout or something because to me it was all bogus crap. I didn't, however, leave the room or do anything to call attention to myself, but during those group sessions, and even during the little intimate family sessions, I always had very mixed emotions.

At the corner of the street where we lived there was a boy who was in the seventh or eighth grade and he and I kind of made friends, I could never REALLY tell because sometimes when he was around friends of his own age he would tease me, so I let him come into my house. I had a hamster back then that was given to me by my now ex-brother-in-law, and one day it got loose in the little TV room that we had. The doorbell rang and I shut the door so the hamster wouldn't get out and went and answered the door. It was that boy so I let him in and we went back into the little TV room.

It was just me home alone with this boy and I got down on my knees and started lifting up couches and things, looking for the hamster. I got down on my knees one particular time with my butt was sticking straight up in the air and this boy asked me, "Do you have any Vaseline?" I immediately stopped my search for the hamster. I got up from where I was kneeling and immediately began running around the house looking for Vaseline because I was hoping he was going to use it for what my brother and me used it for. But unfortunately I didn't find any. While I was looking for the Vaseline he told me he needed to use it on a bruise he had, yeah right because I didn't see a bruise…and I don't know anyone that puts Vaseline on a bruise anyway.

It was around this time that we had found out that my old T-ball coach, Gary Lloyd, was also living in Texas so we decided to pay him a visit. I can recall that day so vividly in my mind because, even though we didn't spend a whole lot of time there and we have since only written to them and have never gone back to their house, that was a day that I had reverted back to my old sexual self.

My parents and both Mary and Gary Lloyd were in the kitchen drinking tea or something like that and talking like grownups tend to do, and I was in the living room, which was clearly visible from the kitchen, with Christopher, who was Mary and Gary's son. Christopher and I were just horsing around and fake wrestling and pillow fighting, you know, things that boys do, when my sexual self decided to show up.

Christopher, who couldn't have been more than nine or ten at the time, dove on top of me as I was sitting down and I, who was at least four years older than him, took this opportunity to do something daring. I grabbed Christopher as he dove at me and I pushed his entire body down on top of my legs so that he was facing the floor, I was sitting Indian style, and I grabbed the shorts and underwear that he was wearing and I pulled them down, taking a look at this little boy's ass. I stared at Christopher, whose butt was up in the air staring straight at me, for what seemed to me to be the longest ten seconds in history.

Christopher got up, pulled his pants up, went over to his dad and promptly said, "Dad, Brad was looking at my butt."

To which his dad said, "You have loose-fitting shorts and you all were playing around, it was probably just an accident." ...That's the first time I ever felt like I could get away with ANYTHING.

When I went to school I quickly got indoctrinated into the high-school way of life in San Antonio. I met a good friend of mine named Armando Almazan, who's nickname was 'Cuckoo', and he was the first REAL goofy person I'd ever met. Cuckoo was always trying to get away with things no one could ever get away with and he was always laughing at one thing or another, which was why I liked him because at this point in my life I needed all the laughter I could get.

I don't remember ever being bullied at this school, oh sure there was teasing and it hurt, but as far as bullying goes there was really none to speak of, which was a very good thing because I'd grown tired of that.

There was, however, one person that did give me a little bit of trouble in ninth grade, and his name was Chris. I would come into English class and I would meet up with him face to face, and he always challenged me by getting up in my face and saying he could beat me up and stuff like that. Well, I was smaller than him so what could I do but take his insults? Chris would pick me up, from underneath my arms over his head, as if to say 'I'm stronger and can beat you up at any time', and try to establish dominance over me. I tried to stay as far away from him as I could, but with us being in the same class it was kind of hard so I just had to tough it out for the rest of the year.

Even though my school had a reputation for being a rough school I was very lucky I didn't experience it first hand. There was a time, however, when I was in the lunchroom and was on my way out to the courtyard when all of a sudden I was being pushed from all sides. I was going out the door faster than I had originally intended, and it was because everybody was scrambling to see a fight that was outside...which I never saw, but I didn't really care.

When I got to my high school I found out that they had lost my records from England so as a result I was held back in a couple of classes. Most notably I was held back in math class because when I had left England I was in pre-algebra, but when I got to Texas and found out that they had lost my transcripts from the other school I was put in a math class called fundamentals of math, which is basically questions like what is 100 plus 100? I was so mad that I was held back, but what could I do? As a result of that I made the best of a bad situation, and coincidentally I was the smartest kid in the class and the one everybody came to for the answers...not so in the next math class which followed in my sophomore year.

In my sophomore year I was put into a math class where all there seemed to be was word problems like, if Judy went south...those kinds of questions. I was never good at word problems for some reason so I barely squeaked by in that class.

My final math class in high school was ironically pre-algebra. When I was put in pre-algebra in my senior year I was very happy because it meant I already knew the material from when I'd taken it in

England so I was well prepared. There were two boys in that pre-algebra class who gave me so much trouble that year and their names were Dietrich, I've forgotten his last name, and Michael Bowman. Both of those boys teased me mercilessly in high school. For example, when I'd be sucking on a lollipop or something one of them would tap me on the shoulder and I would turn around while the other one would be putting tobacco from a cigarette on the end of the sucker. When I turned around and licked it again, I'd get a mouthful of tobacco. I suppose things like that could just be chalked up to kids being kids and that it was the way things were in high school, but I was really intimidated by everyone because of the way people had treated me so when something like that happened to me, I felt very sad and alone and I just wanted them to stop.

On the day of that this lollipop incident I just laughed it off and kept on sucking on it when the bell rang. I don't know whether I felt I needed to prove myself to somebody or something or I just felt like I'd had enough of being pushed around by people, but when the bell rang and my pre-algebra teacher, Mrs. Padron, asked me to throw it away, I looked straight in her face and said, "NO."

Mrs. Padron sent me to the vice principal's office because I had disobeyed her, but I didn't get into too much trouble as a result of what I'd done. However, for some stupid reason I felt very powerful telling someone in authority 'NO'. That was the only time I ever did and I'd wished I'd learned that word in other situations before then.

After that pre-algebra class was done with that year I could have done another year in another math class if I wanted to, but I figured two things: One, I only needed three years of math in high school, and two, I'd finished up here where I finished up in England so that was good enough for me.

I had many people that I knew back in high school that made a little bit of impact in my life; meaning that I can still remember them. Like Priscilla Plaza and Jimmy Covarrubias, who were friends of mine from the time I entered tenth grade until the time I graduated. It was rare for me to have a friend for that long so I relished it. I remember going to our cooking class with them and putting on some awful hairnets and blue aprons and making everything from muffins to cheese balls. I loved being in that class with them because they were so full of humor, for the most part it wasn't educated humor but just goofy stuff that Jimmy would do and Priscilla would always laugh at...she had such an infectious laugh that I just loved to hear it.

There was also a very good friend of mine whose nickname was 'Junior' that I befriended in the tenth grade and I knew him all the way up until I graduated. Junior was a very good friend of mine, the kind of friend that I would lend money to and I never give a second thought about getting it back. I went a whole year giving him money from time to time and never once did I ask for it back, but the very next year he got a job and paid me back every cent in weekly installments...that's class.

During part of 1993 my school was renovating the part of the yard we would walk through to get to the lunchroom so there was a big fence around it, and I manage to get stuck in that fence. My shoe had come untied so I was reaching down to tie my shoe back up and I guess I managed to tie my shoe around the fence because when I got up to go back into the building I couldn't move. There I was, standing there rocking back and forth trying to move away from the fence. I couldn't figure out why I couldn't get away because I didn't know what I had done, and Junior was just standing there laughing his ass off at me trying to walk away, but I kept getting drawn back and slamming into the fence. When something doesn't go right for me I tend to get angry at it instead of thinking it through, and it never dawned on me to look down at my shoes to notice they were tied around the fence. After several minutes of rocking back and forth and junior laughing at me he said, "Dude, I'm just gonna walk away now," and this made me burst out laughing, which made it more impossible for me to concentrate on the subject at hand, which was getting myself loose from the fence. Finally after concentrating on what I was doing and after losing many tears to our laughter I was able to get myself free.

When we moved to San Antonio this time we started out by living in a house where there was the main house and then the garage and then a room built on to it, which became my sister's room. I loved going out to that room because it was so secluded, away from everything else and I felt like I had privacy with my sister that I'd never really had before. I didn't tell her anything about my past, but I liked the feeling of being able to talk to her away from everybody else…to me there was freedom in that.

After we moved back to Texas this time my sister met a man, my parents had a fight with her, and she has never lived at home since. My sister ended up marrying this man, which I thought was cool at first, but it didn't turn out that way. I believe that seeing how my mother and father are is how a marriage is supposed to work, but my sister's didn't go quite that way. I don't remember my mother and father arguing a whole bunch of the time, but that's what my sister and her then husband did. I would go over to his house to watch a pay-per-view wrestling event and all I could hear was them in the background arguing, and I couldn't very well tell them to shut up. I wanted to tell my sister so badly that I didn't like him very much, but in the end I liked my sister too much to cause a rift between me and her so I never said a word.

My brother came home from rehab and it was like he and I continued our 'relationship' right where it left off when we were in England, only this time he had some ammunition to taunt me with. My brother had met a few friends in rehab, I don't know if you could call those people friends, and one of them was named Jerry. Jerry and my brother were, I guess, good friends and I had met Jerry in the rehab clinic. He seemed kind of ok to me and was also kind of cute; I think my brother caught on that I felt that way.

One day when my brother and Jerry were home alone with me, I heard noises coming from my brother's bedroom and I went to see what was going on. These noises sounded of a particularly sexual nature and I asked what was going on in there, to which Jerry shouted out, "Don't come in, we're naked," that was all I needed to hear and then something inside me snapped. I tried anything I could do just to open that door, but I couldn't so I went away disappointed.

My brother used this 'we're naked' tactic several times while he was friends with Jerry, and I fell for it every time. I was never jealous of Jerry though because I knew that after Jerry left, whatever they did together, if anything, my brother would always come back to me to get what he needed.

The frequency of the times when he and I would 'do' each other was almost repulsive to me now because something in him had changed. My brother was now always drunk when he came looking for affection from me, and I was beginning to not like the times that we spent alone together. I began hoping that my mom and dad wouldn't leave us alone together in the house because as soon as they did I knew what he was going to want from me, and by this time in my life I felt I was powerless to say no.

My family had gotten a change to go back to Omaha because of my mother's high school reunion so we all got on a plane and headed back there.

By this time Brandon was a teenager and had filled out a lot more from the last time I had seen him. I had always thought he looked cute, but when I went up to his room where he had his weights and he had his shirt off, all I can remember thinking is how I could get him to start something with me. I asked him if he wanted to wrestle, he said sure and we began rolling around on the floor and on the bed, but I wasn't wrestling him at all, I was feeling every inch of his sweaty body in my hands and loving every minute of it. Brandon and I never did anything, in fact the only thing that I got from him when I got back home and went to the hospital was broken ribs, but I was so hormonal at this point in time that I would have taken any kind of physical contact between Brandon and I.

My sister and brother-in-law's wedding happened at an Air Force base chapel and the wedding reception took place at our house. My grandma on my mother's side flew in for the wedding and reception and it was a treat to have her there. At the reception it was mostly adults except for my brother and me and this other little boy who was brought by a family I don't know, my sister's friends. The boy looked thoroughly unhappy and uncomfortable to be there so I asked him if he wanted to come to my room and play. I also told him that I had a lot of old shirts, which I did, that didn't fit anymore and he could try one on so he could get out of that stuffy dress shirt he was wearing. The boy couldn't have been more than ten or eleven years old and he was all for getting out of that living room where all the grownups were talking about grown-up things like marriage and stuff like that.

I took him into my room and asked him if he wanted to try on a shirt that I had for him. The boy said he definitely wanted to get out of that stuffy shirt so I told him to take his shirt off so he could put the other one on. I just sat there and watched him take his shirt off and when he had it all the way off, I just sat there for a few minutes gawking at this shirtless boy before giving him the shirt I had for him.

I then asked the boy to pull his pants down to which he replied, "Ok." I stood there watching as he was taking his pants down, and when he had them all the way down all I could do was stare at him.

It was time for everyone to go home from the reception so we got out of my room and he went home.

My sister asked me one day, about a couple of weeks after the reception, if I wanted to go to the movies to see *Eraser* with that boy and his sister and I said, "Sure."

We got to the movies and went through the popcorn line before going to sit down. The boy wanted a front row seat so my sister stayed in the middle rows while the boy and I went to sit in one of the front rows. We got to one of the front rows and he sat down next to me. The theater was very packed and there was this other person that wanted to sit down so I asked the boy to sit on my lap so the other guy could sit down. I immediately seized this opportunity to put my hand up the boy's shirt. The boy never questioned what I was doing so I left my hands up his shirt and rubbed his chest, for the remainder of the two-hour movie. I never saw that boy again after that day

The year 1993 was a banner year for me and it would also be a year that changed my life because that was the year that I graduated high school. All throughout that year I had nothing but good times and it seemed like everything was going my way…and it was, it seemed like that for the first time in my life.

Earlier that year, in January, we had gotten our yearbooks and we all were happily walking around from student to student in each class we had getting people to sign them. I walked up to this guy I hardly knew that was in my English class. I knew him a little as we would talk from time to time so we were acquaintances, but not friends. I asked him to sign my yearbook and when I looked down to see what he had signed it said something to the effect of: 'To bad you don't salute the flag, maybe someday you can fight for our country" or something like that. He was referring to a time when we were in English class and the pledge of allegiance came over the intercom, as it had done every day, and I didn't have my hand over my heart. The English teacher Mrs. Grant came over to me while the pledge was playing and placed a hand over my heart…which I thought was VERY cool. The boy, whose name was Juan Carlos Dana, we called him Carlos, never noticed my hand not on my heart before, I don't think, but apparently he had noticed it this time and that's what caused him to write what he did in my yearbook. Carlos and I never talked about what he wrote in my yearbook, but if we had I would have probably told him something like, "I don't put my hand over my heart because I am too busy worrying every day about what me and my brother are going to do after school to give a shit about whether my hand is placed on my heart for two minutes every day or not." On my graduation day I made a special note to myself and during my graduation, when my name was called, I made sure to put my hand over my heart.

My grandma on my mom's side came down for my graduation and I liked that very much. She and I could sit and talk for hours and I loved that about her, and she also told me a couple of things that I didn't know before.

My grandma told me that when I was younger, I think this was in Germany when she came to visit us when grandpa died, and we were playing trivial pursuit that I'd managed to get questions right that she didn't even know, and she told me I was a very smart person. I don't know whether she said that just to see me smile or not. I asked her why she came down to Texas for my graduation, because I didn't think it was anything special, and she told me it was because when I was younger I had asked her that when I graduated could she be there, and she said yes...grandmother's remember the strangest requests from little boys, don't they?

Graduation day for me was so cool because I remember opening all these envelopes and there was all this money inside every one of them...why can't I graduate every day?

After I had graduated I took the summer off and I went to work with my mom. I know it sounds odd that I took time off to go to work, but I didn't look at what I was doing as work because it was more like fun to me.

My mom let me tag along one day to work with her at the Wilford Hall Medical Center Pediatric Clinic and that was a time in my life that changed me forever. I have always loved kids because in England I used to volunteer at a childcare center, but doing what I did at the pediatric clinic was less structured than working with the childcare center. At first when my mom let me tag along it was more, I think, since I didn't have a job I was going to help her out so she had me filing things away and copying things. I even got on the phone and scheduled appointments for people and I was ok with that, but I saw all these kids on the other side of the desk and that was where I wanted to be...so that's where I went.

I met a lot of boys and girls on the opposite side of that front desk and I loved every minute of it. I talked to the older kids about certain things and I would play games with the younger kids; I had a blast. There was one particular day when I didn't go to the clinic and my mother came home and told me that one boy asked where her son was...that was enough affirmation for me and I knew I had found what I wanted to do with my life.

I got several hugs when I was there from the little boys and girls and to me that was what heaven was all about. I befriended a lot of children there as well.

One boy, whose name is Joshua Trotter, actually invited me over to his house to go fishing with him. Joshua gave me his number and I called him a few times...the fishing trip never happened and I was very disappointed, but I was very glad to have known a very special boy named Joshua Trotter.

I was helpful, I think, in many aspects where giving aid to the children were concerned. There were times when I went when they were giving the kids shots and I would hold their hands and comfort them while this was happening, and on several occasions I almost cried from seeing the pain on those kids' faces. There was this one girl that I offered to go with when she was taken to get her shot; she squeezed my hand so hard I swear that she broke, or at least bruised, the bone.

About the same time I was going with my mother to the pediatric clinic my brother had met a girl named Shannon. Shannon was a very sweet girl, at least she was sweet to me; I liked her very much and I wish things had worked out differently.

My brother and Shannon announced one day that she was pregnant and the whole family couldn't have been happier, including me. Shannon and my brother came by one night to the clinic and showed my mom pictures of the ultrasound scan, I took a look at them though and didn't see what all the fuss was about. My brother said that he was moving back to Maryland with Shannon, I guess to be near her parents, and I was very delighted by this news because it meant that I would no longer have to be doing what I was doing with him. Although on the inside it made me kind of sad because I knew what I was when I was around him and now I was losing that.

My dad cosigned a loan for my brother so that he could own a car when he was up in Maryland playing husband and father, that was a big mistake. My brother ended up crashing the car and, of course, with him not having the money to pay for it, the option, well there really was no option, of paying off the car fell to my dad, and that messed up his credit royally.

I remember when my sister-in-law and her dad were down here packing everything up to get ready to move to Maryland. I wanted to wrap my arms around all of them and thank them so much for taking him away and to tell them why I was thankful for them taking him away, but then I thought to myself that if I told them then they might not take him away and I'd be stuck in my all too familiar role.

I was working at the pediatric clinic one day when I saw this little blond-haired blue-eyed boy sitting in the waiting room so I thought I would go over and say 'hi'. His name was Christopher Roberts and he was waiting for his mom and dad to come out of the doctor's office with his sister. I think Christopher must have been ten years old or somewhere around there and I was sitting in the waiting room with him, just basically talking to him and keeping him company until his mom and dad came out, thanked me for watching their son and said goodbye.

Christopher came back the following week and this time it was him that was sick and not his sister. I got very concerned for Christopher and I followed what happened to him very carefully. I went into the room where they give all the shots and things and he had to get a shot in his leg. I remember holding his leg and hiding my face so he wouldn't see my crying and his mother looked at me with that 'It's gonna be all right' face.

I went out of the clinic for just a moment to take something somewhere and when I got back Christopher was nowhere to be found. I frantically asked my mom and the doctor where he went, and they said he had been admitted to the second floor.

I wasted absolutely no time in getting my butt up to the second floor and tracking him down. By this time he already had an IV sticking out of his hand and he just looked so helpless that I couldn't help but go over and give him a big hug. I spent many hours in that hospital room because I loved this little boy so much and I wanted to help him get better. He had to spend his birthday in the hospital, but by the time I found that out it was too late to go out shopping for him so I went down to the hospital gift shop and got him a card and stuck some money inside of it. Christopher was so happy to get that card from me that his face just lit up, and for that moment he forgot he was in the hospital.

There was one time that I will never forget when he had his tray in front of him and he refused to eat. I was so sad that he didn't want to eat that I basically looked at him with kind of a sad face and kept saying, "You have to eat, you have to eat," along with some other words that I don't remember. Eventually he stuck his fork in his food, put it to his mouth and ate it. At that point in time I felt very happy for him for doing that, but I also felt that I could accomplish anything.

The day he was supposed to get out of the hospital I went up to his room and said goodbye and said that I would miss him. His mom asked me if I wanted to come to their house to a birthday party they were going to throw for him because he didn't get a proper one, and I said, "Of course I want to come."

We got to Christopher's house and I spent all of the time that I could with him, and when the cake was ready he sat on my lap and smiled this big smile that I will never forget, I still have the picture even though it is emblazoned in my mind. Christopher and I had so much fun on that day that I was sad to see it end, but I didn't know that more fun with him was just around the corner.

His mom called me one day and asked me if I'd like to go to a softball game, to which I replied, "Sure." I asked if it was a softball game that he was involved in, and she said that it was actually the adults that were going to play and we'd be sitting in the stands on the field.

When we got there it was kind of cold so Jordan, his sister, Christopher and I all stayed in the car. We didn't do much watching of the softball game at all because we were too busy playing and having fun in the car. Christopher and Jordan liked ghost stories so I tried to tell one, miserably, and then it was Jordan's turn to tell hers. She got this blanket from up in the front seat of the car and climbed in the back where Christopher and I were. She then put the blanket over all of our heads and started telling her ghost story.

Christopher was lying with his head kind of on my chest with my hands wrapped around him, and for the first time I felt I knew what non-sexual love was with a boy. Neither Christopher nor Jordan or I heard the key in the car door when it just flung open and their parents got inside. I, for the first time, was scared of the parents seeing the scene with me and their son covered up all the way so you couldn't see what was going on underneath. I thought they were going to think that I was doing something wrong with their son, and I was fully prepared to defend myself, but luckily I didn't have to because they knew nothing wrong was going on; I liked that feeling of trust they had in me. Christopher's parents took me home, I said my goodbyes and I thought I would never see them again.

I walked into the house and immediately started crying, on the inside so no one could see my pain. My mom and my sister were in the kitchen making dinner and I asked them, very frantically, if they could please leave. My sister and mother knew something was wrong and they said that they weren't going to leave and then tried to get me to sit down and talk about anything that was bothering me. I wasn't about to tell them that my heart had just been cut out because I was never going

102

to see this boy that had meant so much to me again…looking back I don't think they realized how much he meant to me and what he represented to me. I took off as fast as I could into my room and turned on my CD player right to the song '*Will You Be There*' by Michael Jackson.

The first time I heard *Will You Be There* was a little before the time when I had to let go emotionally of Zach because his mom couldn't handle that a four-year-old boy and an eighteen-year-old were hanging out together. I had seen the movie trailer for *Free Willy* and I knew I just HAD to go see that movie because the trailer captured exactly how I was feeling, and how I felt about Zach; not in the actions that were going on, but in the words that were being spoken. I went to go see that movie and at the end of it *Will You Be There* was playing, by the time it was over I had tears in my eyes. I identified with *Will You Be There* so much and the message that I received from listening to it that I had to rush out and get a copy of that song wherever I could get it. I rushed right out and bought Michael Jackson's *Dangerous* album because it had the song on there that I had fallen in love with. I can listen to that song now and it puts images into my mind of a time that I felt real and honest love from a child, but back then that song felt SO emotional for me that it ended with bad consequences.

I finished listening to the song, wiped the tears from my eyes so that no one would see how much pain I was in and went into my mom and dad's bathroom; I'd asked if I could take a shower in there and my mom said I could. I had an ulterior motive for wanting to take a shower in their bathroom, I knew I could just as easily have taken a shower in my own bathroom, but this bathroom had something I needed in it...PILLS. I was so sad that I was never again going to see this boy who had meant so much to me that I knew nothing was ever going to be the same again, and I wanted my life over with; I wanted to kill myself.

I went into the bathroom, took off all my clothes and found a bottle of pills. I took the entire bottle then stepped into the shower and tried to wash off the pain I was feeling at losing Christopher, someone that loved me. I got out of the shower and lay down on my bed, waiting for death to come and collect me.

I began to feel really sick. My dad came into my room and wondered what was wrong and that's when I told him I'd taken a whole bottle of pills. He told me he needed to get me to the hospital right away so I agreed and off we went to the hospital, where they flushed out my entire system by giving me this charcoal drink and that made me gag all the pills out of my system.

The doctor came to me and said that physically I was all better, but he wasn't letting me out of the emergency room until I agree to go and see a shrink, so I reluctantly agreed.

It turned out after all that I did see Christopher again because his mom called me and I got to go over to his house one more time, and that's when I told Christopher's mom what I'd done and why I'd done it...that was the last time I ever saw Christopher Roberts.

At the pediatric clinic, working with my mom, at about the same time I met Christopher Roberts, was a lady named Dixie Tulles...her son was very significant in my life. Dixie's son was named Zach and he was no more than four years old and he was one of the best things to happen to me.

I met Zach one day when his family brought Dixie some food. I immediately went over to him and started talking to him like he and I had known each other for a long time. We got to be very good friends in a very short time.

He came over to the hospital again one day with his family, again to bring his mom some food, and we spent about fifteen minutes or so just walking around from doctor's office to doctor's office with him in a piggyback position on my back. We had so much fun we didn't want it to end. I actually got invited to his house on one occasion and I spent the whole day with him and his friends up in a little playroom where the most flattering thing that could ever happen happened to me...Zach never left my side for one minute.

The party was over and we all went home, and one day Dixie told me I could no longer see Zach again and that crushed me so much that I still haven't gotten over it. I did ask if I could see him one last time and she agreed. I thought this was my opportunity to appeal to her. I went right upstairs to Zach's room, and when I got there and tried to explain to him what was going on. He asked me why his mom had said this, to which I replied that I didn't know. Then I put my arms around him to give him a hug and I heard him crying on my shoulder; it almost tore my heart out.

I went downstairs to try to redeem myself in Dixie's eyes, and I asked her why, to which she didn't reply with any kind of answer that I thought was good. I asked her point blank if the Michael Jackson molestation allegations had swayed her in any way and she said it had. She did tell me that Zach didn't want to play with kids his own age anymore because he only wanted to hang out with me, which probably had something to do with it as well.

I left that house without being able to see Zach any more, got into my mom and dad's car and sat in the back with a big coat over my face crying almost out loud. It just so happened that that particular day was the day we went to my weekly psychiatrist appointment. I didn't want to go to the appointment because I knew that we were going to have to talk about my feelings for Zach and I didn't want to do that having just come from his house, but we got into it anyway.

After high school was over and my little stint in the pediatric clinic was over, I was basically lost. I didn't have any clue what to do next with my life and I became very depressed. My brother was no longer around, he was in Maryland with a wife and kid, so I no longer had that routine that I was so used to and missed because by this time it had gone on so long that it had become second nature to me; it was something I was just there to do. The next three years of my life would become both very interesting in some respects and very dull in others, just because I was depressed, that didn't mean I was dead.

I would spend most of those three years in my room listening to my music, pondering my existence and basically feeling sorry for myself. There was really no need for it because there was a world outside my window that I could have taken by storm if I wanted to. I just really had no direction at all and I was drowning in my own self-pity. During the first three years after I graduated from high school I did absolutely NOTHING productive. I did manage to stay very thin during those years because I would just, without much warning, pick up my Walkman and just take off walking to the local mall to just hang out.

I wouldn't say I was an unhappy child because I was the one with all the jokes ALL the time, but I had become an expert at putting things off, not dealing with the pain of what happened and pretending like everything was ok...which I thought it was.

During that period in my life I actually ran away from home twice. One time I ran away I actually was with my mom at the pediatric clinic, something just came over me and I took off. I basically tried to hide in the hospital, weaving in and out of places so my mom wouldn't find me and would give up the search and go home, leaving me to die...I actually wanted to DIE. I made my way to some corridor, some guy spotted me and I tried to bolt when he started asking questions...the end result was that my parents picked me up and we went home.

The second time I ran away I went across the street to a neighbor's house and asked him to take a picture of me so the cops could identify the body when I came up dead. I then took my big boom box and off I went.

I walked about four or five miles on foot until I came to a different neighborhood far away from where I lived and knocked on the door, pleading with this person on the other side to take me in. I don't know what I was thinking because I had very long hair at the time and I hadn't shaved, so who in their right mind was going to take me in, right? He basically told me to get away from his house, in not so nice words.

I kept walking and came to this gas station where I saw a cop car. I pleaded with him to take me to a homeless shelter. The policeman asked me for my name, and fearing that he would take me home, where I didn't ever want to go again, I told him my name was Timothy Dalton. I'm not sure if you know who Timothy Dalton is, but a while back he played James Bond in a few movies. I got my wish and got ushered down to the homeless shelter in the police car; I felt like a criminal. I felt like a criminal because I was running away. I felt like a criminal because I gave a fake name, not just to anyone, but to a police officer. I felt like a criminal mostly because...hello, I was in a cop car.

I got down to that homeless shelter and it was very late so I found a cot and I went to go and lie down. I lay down with my boom box beside me and my headphones on my ears just trying to forget the circumstances that had brought me here because I would worry about that tomorrow, right now I was just happy not to be living my life because, as in the previous time I ran away, I'd come here to die.

I couldn't sleep so I got up from my bunk, it was on the second floor of a two-story building, and I went out on the fire escape because I saw people out there talking. I asked them naively how everything around here worked. They said stuff like you brush your teeth here, you eat over there, you can't stay long here...stuff like that, and I knew I'd gotten myself into a world that I knew nothing about. I wasn't afraid to die, but I was afraid to go through what I had to go through to get there. I lay back down on my cot for about half an hour, and then I promptly went downstairs and made a phone call to my parents.

I went to the Texas Rehabilitation Commission because my parents thought I should DO something so I agreed to go down there and check it out. The Texas Rehabilitation Commission and I talked it over, and I decided what I wanted to do, which was to take childcare courses so I could eventually get a job working with kids. I loved them so much and I now knew now how to love them without thinking of them sexually.

The TRC was going to pay for all of my college (which was amazing to me because I thought my parents would have to pay some out-of-pocket expenses) because I had a sight disability...I HATED the thought of my sight being a disability because to me it wasn't, I had adapted to it.

There I was getting on the bus for my first day of college in hopes of one day being able to work with children in a childcare center environment again when two unexpected things happened to me. One thing that happened was the fact that I rode that bus from one end of the town to the other and back again, I'd missed my stop...I was pissed at staying on that bus for two hours and not getting anywhere.

I eventually got to my classes, and to be honest they went pretty well, and spent the rest of the day just overwhelmed by this big campus and the fact that I couldn't find my way around that easily to any of my classes...but I did it. I had absolutely no problem whatsoever with taking the time out to learn my way to these classes, and maybe stumbling a little bit in finding my way around because I knew eventually I would figure it out. However, the second unexpected thing that happened was what made me rethink my whole reason for being.

I was sitting in class after just taking that long ride on the bus and getting lost, and then trying to find the class I was supposed to be in, in the building I was supposed to be in, and finally settling in, and a realization hit me HARD. I started thinking to myself, *What the hell am I doing trying to be involved in childcare when there is at least one mother out there, Dixie Tulles, who can't stand the thought of me being with her little boy?* I took that one negative instance, instead of all the other positive ones, and made that my blueprint for how others were going to deal with me being around their children.

I immediately went home after classes were over. I had a big discussion with my parents about it and I also told them that I wouldn't be going back to school again. The depression I was going through only deepened at this point because I really felt I had no other place to turn to. I had lost the one thing in the world that mattered to me, which was a career in childcare.

CHAPTER 7:

DECISION TIME

I was sitting at home with my tail between my legs, dejected and depressed, I didn't know what to do with my life so I did the one thing that made sense to me at the time…nothing. Doing nothing seemed like a logical thing to do because, I reasoned, I'd tried doing what I loved to do and failed miserably at that and my brother wasn't around to continue doing what he and I were doing…so in my life, I figured, I had no purpose.

During this time my mother, father and I had moved into an apartment complex. The apartment complex was a weird concept for me because, up to this point, we had always lived in a house...yeah, in Germany we lived in an apartment complex, but to me that was just one big house because we grew to know most of the people in it, and some of them even became like family. This apartment complex was totally different, everybody just did their own thing and nobody got in anybody else's way…kind of lonely I thought.

The apartment complex was where I met another little boy that I will never forget, even though we didn't spend that much time together. I met this boy in the backyard of our apartment, which just so happened to be where the playground was. I went out to that playground several times and during one of those times his mother was out there so we struck up a conversation. I couldn't really tell you what his mother and I talked about, but that was when I actually met the boy known as Chris White. Chris White and I didn't see much of each other in the apartment complex, but when we did we would talk for hours about anything and everything…it was cool.

There was one time when my parents weren't home that Chris came knocking on my door, he had a piece of wood in his hand and said to me, "Let's build something." I agreed, got my dad's hammer and nails and we started to build, truthfully all we did was hammer a couple of nails into the board that he brought over, but it was good enough for us because we got our quality time together.

I recall when Chris came over and told me he was moving because his mom had gotten a job somewhere else; we talked for a while and then we said our goodbyes. I was sad to see Chris leave, but I was getting better with my emotions when it came to children leaving me…or so I thought.

When we were living in the apartment complex, I did try my hand again at training for a career when I went to Career Point Business School. I was going to Career Point to hopefully gain a career in data entry. I HATED the fact that you had to go dressed in business attire. When I arrived at the school I had to be dressed in slacks, dress shoes, and a tie...to me that sucked. I agreed to do it and went to that school for about four or five weeks, or something like that, and then, I don't know why I did this, but I quit Career Point Business School and have never gone back since.

My sister worked at Chelsea's Street Pub, which was a very popular place in the local mall to eat and drink that I frequented very often. I had a problem with the skimpy (it looked to me) shorts that they made her wear in that place, but because I was four years younger than her, plus the fact that she was married and able to do whatever she wanted, I really had no control whatsoever over the situation.

At this point in my life I wasn't doing anything at all as far as a job was concerned so I took these opportunities to visit my sister as often as I could. I couldn't see very well so driving was out of the question; glasses were no help at all because to me they made everything clearer, but they also made everything smaller so really what was the point? My parents weren't available so how was I going to get to the mall where she was?

I had been walking since 1989 when my mom said, "Ok now that your high school is within walking distance that means I no longer have to take you so you are going to walk." I had a Walkman because I enjoyed music SO MUCH. Music has been my way of communicating what I seem to have a hard time saying out loud. One day I just took off walking to the mall, and I continued doing that for quite some time. It was around fifteen miles from where we lived to where my sister worked, but I didn't mind the walk at all because as long as I had my music with me I could have walked till the batteries ran down and I wouldn't have cared. I would have cared if the batteries ran down while I was still walking, then the walk would have seemed like forever.

Once inside the mall I would immediately head for Chelsea's Street Pub and sit down in the section I thought my sister was going to be serving in, sometimes I'd ask. The times that I spent there with my sister were good times because, although she was working, she would take time out to come and chat with me and introduce me to her friends that she worked with. I liked that because it validated me as something more than I thought I was.

They have long since torn down Chelsea's Street Pub, but I will always remember the pub because those were some of the best times I spent with my sister, whom I love so much, and my Barbeque

Cheeseburger.

The way I hear it from my sister-in-law is that he was still using drugs and drinking so she kicked my brother out. The way I hear it from other people is that my sister-in-law used him in some way and then kicked him out; either way he got kicked out of the house for one reason or another. I had yet to find this out from anyone.

I was sitting on the couch one day just minding my own business while watching TV or something like that when my mom came over and said something to me that totally shocked me, and I have yet to get that familiar phrase out of my head or the feelings it conjured up. My mom came up right beside me as I was sitting on the couch and said, "Your brother is coming home." 'Your brother is coming home', to me, was the worst thing anyone could have ever said because I'd already been there and done that and now I was going to have to go through it all over again. I didn't let anybody see the worry on my face or show any kind of emotion whatsoever to let people know that something was terribly wrong, but I should have because I wasn't at all prepared for how bold my brother was going to be.

The day that my brother came back to live with us, only temporarily while he found a place to live, was a day that I will never forget because during that night I found out just how bold a person he could be.

The day started off just like any other normal day, me AGAIN not doing anything and hiding behind a wall of depression, and my parents helping my brother move back home. It was late and time for us all to go to bed after a long hard day of getting everything in the house situated. We all went upstairs, except for my brother who didn't have a bed because up until that day no one knew he was going to live there, and said our goodnights. I stayed up for a little while watching TV or listening to music or something, but no sooner had I turned out my light than there was a knock at my door.

I opened my door and found my brother on the other side. He said he wanted to talk so I went downstairs with him. I could smell the alcohol on his breath, and I knew what he was going to want when we got downstairs, but I was kind of 'ok' with the fact that he probably wanted me just to suck him off...I was prepared for that.

My brother looked me straight in the face and said, "Fuck me."

I told him, "I can't, Mom and Dad might here the noise and come down." I can't believe that I was trying to plead with my drunken brother about whether to fuck him or not.

When the drama of the night was over I went back up to my bedroom and fell asleep. When I awoke it was like nothing had happened the night before.

This house was the last house my brother ever touched me sexually in, and although the physicality was gone between him and I, it manifested itself in very unhealthy ways...like doing what I did with my own brother was healthy, right?

My family didn't spend a very long time in that apartment complex, just about a year, or maybe less. My father, mother, and I soon moved into an actual house again, which we rented, just about twenty minutes from where we had previously lived. To tell you the truth I was glad to get out of that two-story apartment because I hated the fact that another family was living just a wall away from us, I don't know why I did, but I just hated that.

We next moved into a house that was just perfect for me because the numbers on the address were 1234, I guess my parents figured that this way I could always find my way home. We moved in about 1995 or early 1996 and in that house is where I believe I actually, finally, got to do a little growing up. When I say I got to do a little growing up I mean that when I was younger everything was all just talking about sex, thinking about sex, wondering about sex, and of course the actual act of sex. Yet NOW, semi-free from my brother, he still hung out with us at least once a week when he needed his laundry done or something, I was able to try and get that out of my system and focus on better things; but I still had a hard road to pave.

Throughout 1995 I didn't do much of anything but hang out in my room, listen to music, and take lots and lots of walks. There is one walk I took that I will never forget.

I was in the local arcade playing video games when I looked at my watch and said to myself, 'Ok, you've spent enough time here, now it's time to go home." I was on my way home from the arcade, at almost nine o'clock at night, when about three quarters of the way home I was crossing a little side street and a car stopped and this, I found out later, thirty-year-old man asked if I wanted a ride home. I said, "Ok." I got inside the man's car and we proceeded to drive in the direction where my house was, but I got a little worried when we went past it, but I really didn't say much.

He started making a little small talk with me and then he asked me "What are you into?"

I said, "What do you mean?"

He said, "Are you into basketball?"

And I said, "No, I'm into wrestling and video games."

The next question he asked clued me into what he really wanted.

The man, staring at the road and concentrating on where he was taking me, asked me if I was into guys...while his hand started rubbing my dick.

This man took me to his apartment and before we even stepped out of the car it was like a switch went off in my head. Now I was ready for whatever he and I were going to do together. The man did something that I didn't count on and it ruined what could have been just 'another day at the office' for me, so to speak. The man went over to his dresser and turned on some music, and that somehow brought the whole situation for me from what I thought it was into something that I knew I didn't want...it humanized the situation, and that made me freeze up. That man did do something that no other person had done to me before...he put a condom on me. I don't know about everybody else, but to me a condom is a very intimate piece of equipment that is only shared between two people who are 'in love', and I DEFINITELY wasn't that way with someone I had just met that night.

In about the middle of 1996 my dad saw an ad in the paper because he needed some extra income at the time, and he asked me to take a look at it and said I should go apply there with him. I went with him to apply and we both got the job; it was the best month that I ever spent at a temporary job. I got to get out of the house and actually be with other people instead of at home brooding about things I couldn't possibly change. I got the chance to strike up friendships with some people who were very kind to me. I got the chance to make money and pay for things that I wouldn't normally have gotten...which was sometimes a bad thing.

With one of my paychecks I went out and bought a Web TV, and

I could tell you now that I, at twenty-one, wasn't ready for it and got into a lot of trouble with it. I was able to find pictures that I didn't have any business looking at, and WebPages that I should never have been on. Even though I was old enough chronologically to be looking at them, emotionally and psychologically I was still nothing more than a little child, and putting that kind of power into a little child's hands that looks very much like an adult can be very damaging. I did a lot of talking on the Web TV chatroom about sex, and things I would do for anyone that wanted to do anything with me. I met some interesting people online and one of them was a thirteen-year-old boy. I'd lied about my age and said I was thirteen as well.

We started chatting about the things we liked and the normal things that gay teens talk about, size, how often you jack off, things like that. We started talking to each other on a regular basis over the Internet and we agreed we wanted to meet someplace; he wanted to call me first though. We talked a lot on the phone and it sounded like he was very comfortable with talking to me, but then towards the end of everything the kid had doubts and thought I was lying to him even though I tried to persuade him that I wasn't, but we never did meet and that was the end of that. My motives weren't pure at all, in fact they were downright sick, but that's all I knew about the way to behave and how I was SUPPOSED to be, so that's what I did.

There were a few other online experiences that I will never forget to this day. There was a time when I went into a chatroom one day and I saw two teenagers who lived in two different states talking about how, when one of them was going to visit the other's state, they were going to get together so they could have sex. I said I wanted in on it so we could have a three-way...and they agreed. The three-way never came off, but that didn't stop me from getting the love I thought I was missing.

My next stop on the Internet trail to disaster was when I chatted with this guy who was thirty years older than me...he was fifty. When I met him in the chatroom we started talking for a little while and at first I had no idea how old he was, but when I did the idea didn't turn me off at all because at least it meant someone would love me like I knew how to love. I pretended that I had stuff to do and told him I would meet him at the local mall.

I took off for the mall to meet this guy and hung out for a while until I got to the designated meeting place, and then I saw him coming straight at me. He asked me if I would like something to eat and he would pay for it, which I thought was creepy because I thought he just wanted to do what we met each other for. He told me he was a professor at some local college and that no one knew about his sexual preferences...who the hell was I going to tell?

We got done eating and drove almost to where my house was, and then he stopped and parked the car. He did something to me that I thought no one, besides my brother when we were younger, would ever do...he stuck his tongue in my mouth. To most, probably, the thought of someone thirty years older than yourself shoving their tongue in your mouth is probably the grossest thing you could ever think of, but to me it was a robotic thing...he started going for my mouth and I knew what he wanted so I gave it to him.

He then proceeded to unzip my pants and slide them down. He slid my pants down just enough so that he could get to my dick and then he sucked it. We talked about going to his house, but we never did actually get there and the night ended with him taking me to the street where I lived and me walking the rest of the way home.

The last Internet experience that I had was an experience that I'm very glad I didn't fulfill because I have a feeling my life would have been very different had I fulfilled it. I got to talking with this guy who said he came to my town frequently on business and he wanted to know if I wanted to 'hook up' with him; I said sure.

He started telling me about a bathhouse that he went to a lot where the men all took their clothes off, got into robes and basically walked around naked except for those robes on. The man also told me about when the guys went inside private rooms and what happened when the robes came off. The guy went on to tell me that frequently someone could just come in the room where you were and join in the fun, which sent my mind racing in all kinds of directions. I was more than happy to go there with him and do the things that he was talking about, but when he said for me to meet him there it was like the whole bathhouse situation suddenly took on a life of its own and I didn't want to do it anymore.

I talked to him online and told him I was thinking about not going but still hinting that I might go, but he was kind of mad and finally I ended up chickening out and not going at all.

Part of me wonders what would have happened had I gone to that bathhouse, and then there's another part of me that kind of knows how it would have turned out and that I should be very glad that I didn't go.

At the end of 1996 and beginning of 1997 I again had no job and I really wasn't looking for one at all...I was STILL in deep depression mode and didn't care much what happened to me. Near the beginning of 1997 my parents thought I should be involved with 'Lighthouse for the Blind' and somehow they would be able to help me get a job. I never did like the whole connotation of Lighthouse for the Blind because I certainly didn't need it because I didn't feel like I was handicapped in any way.

Every day that I went to Lighthouse was like hell for me because here I was being taught stupid stuff like how to screw a nut to a bolt, if anyone knew how to screw something…it was me. And then when it came to lunchtime I would go into this big lunchroom where hundreds of people walked around with dark glasses and canes…it was just an environment that I felt ill equipped and uneasy about being in. I couldn't wait to have any excuse to get out of that place so when it came time for lunchtime again I wasted no time in finding someplace down the street where I could go eat and get away from the uneasiness of my situation.

When I got through with all the testing at the Lighthouse it brought me no closer to getting a job than when I went in there to begin with. However, the Lighthouse for the blind did make a suggestion to me; they said I should try Easter Seals.

Before I got into the Easter Seals program I decided to take a trip down to my former shrink. I went on seeing my shrink for a while, telling him more and more that I hadn't told him previously and he put me on some antidepressant medication. I want to state here and now that I don't put any stock into antidepressant medication because I believe for some people it's not a chemical imbalance that makes them depressed but having to deal with situations that they haven't dealt with properly; this is what does it.

Easter Seals was a place that said they would guarantee to get me a job, and that was good enough for me because I wasn't going to actively seek one out. I started going through their program. It's a place where people on medication, it seems like, go to get reacquainted with the world of work, and I started meeting the people there and it wasn't at all half bad once I got into it.

I even met a guy named Jason Guerrero, who was the first person I actually told things to. Jason was plump, but he was very sexy to me, I think I will be forever in my 'look at 'em as sex objects' mode. When I first saw him all I wanted to do was to get him alone and see if he wanted to do anything with me.

The first day I met Jason we talked a little, walked down to the bus stop together and he invited me over to his house. We instantly hit it off like we had been friends for a long time, even though we only started talking that very day.

Jason and I got to his house and he took me in his back bedroom so he could change, that's where I told him some stuff that had happened to me. In the middle of changing he said that if him changing in front of me was uncomfortable for me, then he would stop…which I thought was totally sweet of him to say. I told him, "No, it's ok," and he continued changing. However, when he took his shirt off my robotic mind took over and all I could see was his naked chest.

Jason and I went out into the front room, where our pizza was waiting, and sat down to have some lunch. I told him more about what had been done to me, and I also told him that I was attracted to him. Jason said that he was flattered and that he would stop it if it went too far.

We started talking some more until I put my arms around him and cried like a little baby because it seemed like everything at that moment could come out. I'd never told anybody anything about what had happened in my past, but now that I had I felt this tremendous weight lifting from my shoulders; I was finally free.

I said, "Jason, you look tense, would you like a massage?" He said ok and I was able to put my arms around this sexy guy's shirtless body, and I only felt a twinge of sexual thought. I was so mad at myself because he was sitting there ready for me to make a move, ready for me to do what I've done all my life, and I just couldn't do it...I felt so mixed up inside.

He took me to one of his church meetings that night. He took me to several of his church meetings, but I told him many times that I didn't know if I believed in that stuff and that I was just there for the purpose of seeing him. He understood, but thought that with me there some of the stuff that they were teaching might sink in…it didn't. Our little friendship's downfall was when I played the 'using me' card. I went right up to him and told him to take his dick out, basically stop fucking with me, and that was the beginning of the end.

I don't know what possessed me to tell my parents some of what had happened between my brother and I, but that was a day that I'm still living to regret.

I called my mother in to my room and told her that my brother had molested me. She and I had a little discussion about that and I kind of felt good that I'd told her, but that feeling didn't last long at all. The next time I went to see my shrink, at this time me and my parents were involved in group discussions as well as just me and my shrink, my mother just blurted out to me, in front of my psychiatrist, to tell him what happened between me and my brother. You could have heard a pin drop as I was staring at her with mad penetrating eyes when she brought that up to a man who wasn't in the family fold.

I told my shrink what happened between me and my brother and two things happened that I couldn't have foreseen. One of the things that happened was the fact that my mom couldn't handle what I'd told her for whatever reason, and she got admitted to the psychiatric ward in the hospital. The next thing that happened was that I was instructed to go and see someone that dealt with sex crimes, sexual feelings, and things of that nature.

When I told my parents what had happened to me I was thinking that they took the news pretty well, yeah there were questions to be answered, but all in all I felt it was a good discussion. A short time after I told my mother what had happened she went to the psychiatric ward in the hospital. She came back home after spending what I thought was very little time there, and I asked her what had caused her to go to that place. My mother told me that what I had said to her had brought back feelings of what had happened between her and her own brother. All I heard in that sentence of 'It brought back what happened between me and my brother' was that it was MY FAULT that she'd ended up in the psychiatric ward.

There have been a lot of people in my life that have told me that it wasn't my fault, but as soon as those words came out of my mother's mouth…it was FOREVER my fault. My life with my mother has never been the same since she said that to me. I took it as blame because once she started going to a shrink herself to deal with those issues, to me it was like she ceased to want to do anything anymore. Since her initial visit she has been up to the psychiatric ward so many times that I have lost count. When my mom was the mother I knew back then, she was good to me, helped me out with problems and she was there for me when I needed her, but now all she seems to want to do is sleep all the time. She says it's because of the medication she is taking for several different things, and while I will agree all those medications can probably take you on a lot of ups and downs, I think it is more that she has lost that zest for life and doesn't see the point anymore.

I did as I was told and went to this 'sexuality shrink' or whatever the hell he was called, and we talked a lot about sexual preference and things like that. I basically told him that I didn't know what sex I preferred and that I only knew what I'd been taught. I told him I liked young boys, but had never really explored fully the reason why I did, which probably has a hell of a lot to do with my past. We talked some more about how it feels when I'm with a young boy, which I didn't delve into all that much because he knew nothing about my past except ONE instance with my brother that I told my other shrink about. I went to this guy for four or five weeks, or something like that, and he came up with a scenario that to this day I don't know whether is true or not. He said, "It sounds to me like you don't even want to change so I can't help you." I would tell him one minute that I did want to change, that I didn't want to be the way that I was and have the feelings that I had, and in the next minute I would be telling him something totally different…I was a contradiction.

When my mom, dad, and I went to see my psychiatrist, not the sex doctor, and I was basically forced by my mom to tell him what had happened between my brother and I, what she knew anyway, my mom had a reaction that I didn't anticipate. My mom got real red in the face and heated and told me, not in the privacy of our own home but in front of a stranger, that she wasn't going to allow me anywhere near Timmy…my brother's son. I thought that this statement was a little ironic because of what my brother had done to me, the ONE time I told her about and the others that she didn't know about, but I figured that she was entitled to her own opinion, whether right or wrong. In the psychiatrist's office I played it real cool like I really didn't care what she had to say, but that day stung me in the heart in more ways than one. Even though I never showed it I was angry with her for ever thinking I would do anything to my nephew. I was horrified that she was more worried about the fact that she didn't want me near my nephew and not the fact that my nephew's father, my brother, was doing this stuff with me…even though she only knew of one time. This one statement by my mother also basically solidified my 'nobody wants me around children' attitude.

I continued going to Easter Seals through all this drama that was being played out, which had now become my life. I was really more lost than ever before and I decided to quit the medication the doctor had put me on cold turkey. When you go on anti-depression medication and you decide to come off of it cold turkey…it's not a good idea. I crashed and burned big time, inside the front door of Easter Seals I just got down on the floor in a fetal position and start crying like a baby as loud as I could. The people and staff that were around me tried to help as best as they could, and I really thanked them for that, but I felt no one could handle this downward spiral but me.

I continued hanging out with Jason Guerrero for a little while after that, in fact he was one person that was instrumental in making me feel needed and loved. To tell the truth though, I didn't really like who I was because of the fact that I liked Jason so much. I became dependant on Jason in a way; I would go where he went and do what he did just for the sake of hanging around him, partly because I liked him and partly because I didn't want to be alone and have to face my demons alone...I was messed up.

I finished my stay at Easter Seals with a job that I could be proud of having, the first job that Easter Seals wanted to throw at me was as a janitor and I said, "No Way!" I was going to go back to the job I had before. Easter Seals had gotten me a job with the same company I had worked for before, rhymes with Spears but take out the P, and I was back on my way towards gainful employment. Only I didn't know how much it was going to cost me in the end, but I found out almost eight years later when I lost my best friend and my job at virtually the same time.

When I started working at this place I didn't treat it as a job, to me it was just some place to go that wasn't home that just happened to be paying me for being there. When I started work there the dress code was slacks and a tie, I hated that, but other than that it was a very relaxed atmosphere and I really liked working there.

My very first supervisor was someone I'll never forget because, although he hadn't known me that long, he stuck up for me in a way that I'll always remember. I was on the phone with this very difficult customer and they wanted to speak to my supervisor so I handed the phone over to him. After my supervisor got done talking with him he said, "I'm going to put you back with the consultant now," and then I heard my supervisor say, "No, he's a very competent person," and then the phone was handed back to me. From the conversation and what my supervisor said I gathered that the customer didn't think I was very competent and when my supervisor contradicted him and stuck up for me like that it made me feel real good inside. It wasn't that he would just stick up for me, but the fact that he'd called me a competent person made my self-esteem skyrocket. Wherever that guy is now, I know that he must be doing great and I wish him all the best that life has to offer. That first supervisor also gave me something for Christmas that I will always cherish to this day...*The Jackson Five Ultimate Collection* CD.

I had many supervisors in my almost eight years at that place and I opened up to some of them as well. I think I talked more in that place to more people about what I've been through than I've ever talked to anybody in my life, it was like that place was a safe place for me where I could just unburden myself. All of the people that I've told things to have been very kind and understanding people, one or two have even tried to help me by suggesting I go back to a psychiatrist…I loved them for wanting to help me.

Halfway into my eight years of working there I met this woman named Maria Garcia, who liked to be called Linda. Linda was about twenty years older than I was and I think she was a little infatuated with me because one day we ended up walking to my house. It was raining pretty hard, I LOVED it, and we just took off walking in the rain. Linda was talking about getting in where it was dry and maybe calling my dad, but I wouldn't hear of it because the rain felt good to me.

We were walking along the side of the street when my dad pulled up beside us and told us to get in, which we did. My dad was talking to us about us being out there when it was pouring down with rain. Linda and I were in the backseat, there was no one in the front, but I thought it was just polite to sit back there with her, and her hand found its way inside mine. I didn't really think all that much about it. But when we got to my house and I took her to my room and shut the door (I have this thing about shutting my door, and even locking it sometimes, when I'm in there) she expressed a little of her feelings. I remembered back when I expressed feelings to Jason so I was able to pretty much treat it as a friendly type of thing.

We would always go out to eat at the mall, talk at work and walk home from work sometimes when her car wasn't available to her...it was fun. She was a devout Jehovah's Witness and she would talk to me sometimes about it. She started saying stuff like we couldn't hang out together if I didn't believe what she believed in, which I thought was nonsense, but I couldn't change what she thought any more than she could change what I thought.

The last day we hung out together was the day I decided to let my guard down and tell her what I'd been through in my life, not as a way of keeping her beside me, but it was just that something inside me told me to tell her.

It was time for us to get off work, about five or so, and she offered to give me a ride home. We both got in her car and settled in for the ride home...only we didn't get home until the next morning. We got in her car and started shooting the breeze about this or that, we could talk for hours about anything, and it just seemed like out of the blue I brought up what had happened to me. I talked for a good twenty minutes about myself and every time I looked up at her she had a glassy look in her eyes.

I finished telling her my life story and she did something that I don't believe anybody has ever done when I got done telling them about me...she hugged me. Linda didn't just give me one of these 'I'm sorry it happened' hugs, she gave me one of these turbo hugs that lasted at least ten minutes, maybe more. I could hear her crying behind my shoulder so I just held her in my arms for the longest time.

When I asked her what got her so upset she confessed to me that she hadn't dealt with what happened between her and her brother. Finally everything made sense to me and I knew why these things had happened to me...it was so I could help others deal with their pain. That was the last day we hung out together, her call not mine.

There were many people I met at my career at Spears, take away the P, all of the experiences I had there were great and I wouldn't change a single one. One friend, on my birthday, actually brought in a cake that she had bought for me, which I thought was so sweet that I almost cried.

There was one year out of my life that I would definitely like to relive again and that was the year I met a little ten-year-old boy named David Morgan Woolverton.

I met a woman named Linda Woolverton while working for a special department in the company I was working for at the time, and she seemed pretty nice to me. We didn't talk that much at first when I started working for that special department. Linda started telling me about her family and how she wanted to do something special for her son for Christmas. She'd heard I knew how to turn blank CDs into ones with music on them so she asked me if I could help her with that because she wanted to give her son a stereo for Christmas. I said I had no problem with that so we made up a story about how I was going to give my nephew some CDs for Christmas. He was about David's, Linda's son, age and I needed David's opinion on what CDs I should give to my nephew...all the while I would just be giving the CDs to David's mom to give to David.

David and his mom came over to my house one night and I felt an instant connection with David at that moment, I knew right at that very moment that David and I were going to be more than just two people who knew each other.

I made those CDs for David and Christmas time had rolled around, I don't know if it was me or Linda, but we decided I should come down and give him the CDs personally. I went down to David's house, from now on that's what I'll call it, gave the CDS to him and was getting ready to leave when he suddenly came over to me and gave me the biggest hug I could have ever received. I have to say that I almost started crying right there because, up until Zach Tulles, I had never received that kind of love from a boy before, and I liked it very much.

After receiving a hug from him and knowing what that felt like I knew I was hooked, and I wanted to stay around this boy for as long as possible. I discussed the hug with Linda and she said she felt good about it.

I walked every single day to work, but when I started seeing David I decided to go down to his house and get a ride from his mom into work since we both came in at the same time. I loved going there every day and spending time there before I went to work because I would play games with David or we would just talk...it was great, and David loved it.

The first time I sang to him was a day that I came over just to hang out with him. I taught him how to download songs off the Internet and we downloaded a Michael Jackson song called

Speechless. David had a very slow Internet connection so it took about a few days for him to download it, but when it did download I sat there with him on my lap, pressed play and sang along with the words directly to David. Then I gave him a big kiss on the cheek.

Speechless is such a beautiful song and I wanted to share its sentimentality with him. I also taught David how to do voicemails over the computer. I always believe in telling a child you love them every time that you see them and David was no exception, that is why I was so pleasantly pleased, and very touched, when EVERY SINGLE voicemail he sent me from his computer said I LOVE YOU at the end of it. There is nothing sweeter in this world than when you hear a child say 'I love you'.

David and I continued our singing when he would come down to my house when I was off from work. The second song I ever sang to him was a Tina Turner song called *Whatever You Want*, and I meant every word that I sang to him.

There was a time when David wasn't doing so hot in school and Linda told me to express to him that I didn't like it, only she had me telling him that I was so mad with him I wasn't going to come down there for a while, which I reluctantly went along with. Linda sent me a note basically the same day, or maybe it was a day after, saying that David had set his alarm to speak with her about seeing me again and he made reference to the song that I sang to him and said, "That's what I need, mom, I need Brad."

Linda asked me what I thought about it and of course I came down the very next day and patched things up with him, but I felt very uneasy about the way I thought Linda had played us both. I ended up telling her most of the stuff that had gone on in my life, I felt it only fair because I was friends with her ten-year-old boy, so the fact that she agreed to what she agreed to really made me very happy.

The year that I met David will be a birthday I will never forget. I asked David's mom if David had ever had a sleep over because I heard his sister talking about ones that she'd had, and she either said no or not very many, and I got this great idea in my head if he could have a sleep over with me.

The day he came over to my house to spend the night David did something so shocking to me that I will never forget it. This ten-year-old boy actually baked a cake for me, I had no idea how to cook and this little boy had baked a cake for me. I was almost in tears it was such a sweet thing to do. His mother told me not to say anything about the fact that it was kind of flat because his sister had laid her schoolbooks on it or something...the cake looked PERFECT to me.

That night my parents took us out for my birthday dinner at IHOP, we had a lot of laughs and I'm glad David was there to be a part of the fun. Our drinks came and David leaned in to take a sip of his soda and the soda tipped and landed with a little bit of it on the table, but the rest of it landed in David's lap. You should have seen his face when that ice-cold beverage landed there, his face was so funny, and I thank David for making my mom laugh like that. David scrambled to clean it up as best he could and went into the bathroom to dry off.

When he came out we finished our meal with him having to eat with a wet lap. After we got done eating we got up to leave and went out to the parking lot. My dad opened the car door and was looking around for a bag or a towel for David to sit on before he got in the car. David asked what my dad was doing and my dad said, "You have to sit on something," and wouldn't you know David looked straight at me with this 'how about on him?' look.

I looked at him and said, "No way."

David was such a funny person. We stayed up that night for a while and I put in the movie *Free Willy* for us both to watch, I watch it every year on my birthday, and he was falling asleep on the floor while watching it so I told him, "Let's just go to bed."

We didn't go right to bed because his mom wanted us to go online chat with her when she got home from work and I agreed, so we just stayed up a while and chatted until it was time to get on the computer and talk to Linda.

We got through talking to Linda and went into my room to go to sleep. I gave David my bed while I slept on the couch that was right next to the bed. We held hands, said 'I love you', and then had just started to drift off to sleep when David asked me if I could come join him in the bed. I scooted over and joined him, putting my arms around him so he would feel safe, until a few minutes later when he was fast asleep and his arm landed square in my face; I decided it was time to move back to the couch.

I was still into wearing very dark clothes back then, not so much anymore, and every time I went over I would have on black shorts and a black shirt. I would knock on David's door and he would say, "Here's Brad wearing black again," or words to that effect. I thought what David was saying was just to tease me or something so I never really paid any attention to it, but his mom said that he and his sister were very worried about me wearing dark clothes when it was nighttime. Had I heard straight from David or Jessie that me wearing dark clothes bothered them, I probably would have changed and not worn dark stuff around them, but because I'd had, even at an stage, an uneasy feeling about their mom, I didn't even give it a second thought.

I'm thoroughly convinced that David's mom didn't like the fact that I was getting so close to him, and several times she tried to make me start an argument or something with her so she could make our relationship end. Linda Woolverton has, unfoundedly, called me a liar on several occasions.

The first time she called me a liar was when I went down to David's house to play with the games he got for Christmas. My dad came to the door and asked me to go to Sears with him so we could get some new tires. Linda, later on that night, asked me what had pulled me away from David, and I said that my dad had taken me to Sears to buy some tires, but she said I wasn't telling her the truth. I went so far as to ask my dad for the receipt for the tires; I copied them and was prepared to take them down so she could see them, but she said she didn't need to see them when I told her I had them…she never apologized.

Another time she accused me of lying was when our specialty team was closing down and half of us got put on another specialty team and half of us didn't. I was part of the half that went on the new team and she was in the other half, but she accused me of knowing that I was going to be on that team and not telling her about it when I really had no prior knowledge of what was to happen. Linda said, "Come on, you had to have known, you aren't that naïve." I wanted to smack her for saying that. I never once called her on the carpet in front of her kids for calling me a liar, I would never do that to anyone, but sometimes I wanted to.

There have been two times that I gave Linda money because she called me and told me about the fact that her husband had medical problems and she didn't know how she was going to pay those bills on top of getting the kids things that they needed and wanted. I was more than happy to do what I could for those kids so I gave her the money without any thought of ever getting it back. I think that's what you should do if you are ever going to give money.

The one thing that shocked me about that whole giving her money experience was that after I had given her the second dose, so to speak, her friend Dorothy from work called me and said, "Linda said I should call." And then she asked me for money to pay for her application fee for a new apartment she was going to be renting.

Throughout my life I have been known to be generous with certain things, and without making much of a fuss and I did give Dorothy the money, but I have to tell you that I was pissed at Linda for doing that to me…although I never did verbally beat her up for it.

David and I played hard during that year that I knew him and we hung out a lot, sometimes at my house, sometimes at his house, but every time we hung out together it didn't matter what we did because it was all great. I don't know if I pushed it on David or he liked it, but we sang a lot. I showed David some dance moves and he would even get up and dance to the music with me, and sometimes he would just lie there on the bed and stare at me while I sang to him. I had to be careful what I sang to David because if there was a song with the word 'girl' in it, he'd accuse me of calling him a girl, he was such a funny guy, but I tried to leave out those songs whenever I could. I made sure the songs that I sang to him and the ones that he learned from me had a positive message so that he would come away from having known me as a more enlightened child.

I'll never forget when we went out to a baseball game courtesy of tickets that Dorothy won for selling well at work. David came over to my house that night and I don't know if he didn't like the shirt he was wearing or if it was a good shirt and he didn't want to get it dirty but he asked me if he could look in my closet for a shirt to wear. I said 'sure' and we were off to the game.

I couldn't really tell you what happened at the game or who won because we seemed to be spending all of our time getting drinks and food and gifts…which was all right with me because I would have given him anything he wanted.

We finished watching the game and got into my dad's car, I always let him sit up front, and he was telling my dad what we bought. He said, "We both got silver balls."

My dad, without missing a comic beat said, "Boy, you are manly men" or something like that.

I just said, "Daaad," because I couldn't believe he said that to a ten-year-old boy. I don't think David got it because he didn't laugh.

There were two times that I learned from his mother that he'd lost his temper and beaten up his sister, one that I was able to do something about. The first time that I heard that David had beaten his sister up I went right down to his house and I let him know, in no uncertain terms, that I was upset with his actions, I think I actually raised my voice at him…something I try never to do with a child. I taught David the meaning of respect that day and told him that I could never respect someone who did that to a girl, let alone his sister. I think he got the message because he apologized for doing it. I was told by his mother that I'd taught him good manners; but that she hated the fact that now when she called him he answered with "yes ma'am".

The second time I was told that David had beaten up his sister I was forbidden to discuss it with him by his mom because David had told her not to tell me. Presumably he knew how hard I would come down on him for doing it. If he knew she'd told me, then he would never have trusted her again...those were his words, she said. In retrospect I probably should have told him that I knew about it because that would have caused him to not trust his mother, and maybe I would still be hanging around with him today...but I am NOT the vindictive type.

I don't know where the beginning of the end came between David and I, but I can tell you that at the root of it was the fact that I thought I was losing him because of his getting bad grades and not being able to come over. And after all I felt I'd been through, losing him was the LAST thing I wanted to happen after finding love. I started basically becoming a pest and asking why David couldn't come over. I was essentially bartering with Linda, telling her that I would make sure he got good grades if he was able to come over to my house. I tried to do anything and everything to get him to be able to come back to my house. I thought I had succeeded when his mom said he could come over if I would tutor him and make sure he got help with his homework.

I was all set for the day that he was able to come over to my house to get help with his homework, but it didn't pan out and I became very depressed about it. I began pestering Linda again about him coming down. While this was going on Linda said she went online one night and she said I said something that she found very offensive and she was mad at me now. I contend I never went online and therefore NEVER said anything bad to her. I asked her what I had said that was bad, but she pulled out the famous 'you know what you said' speech. I was so mad at this I just wanted to tell her, 'Look, if I knew what I said then why would I be asking you what I said?' Of course I would have been more colorful because that's how mad I was.

Linda went for days without speaking to me and prior to that we had sent emails back and forth to each other. However, sometimes I felt her emails were filled with hostility, and now that she wasn't talking to me based on something she never told me that I had said, I felt I had no choice but to get to the bottom of things. I couldn't get to the bottom of things by talking to Linda because she wasn't talking to me at the time, and for some reason I felt I couldn't go to her husband so I did the next best thing I could do; I went to her kids for advice.

I printed out several emails that she and I had sent back and forth to one another and took them down to her kids with the intention that they would read them and try and help me find out what Linda was so mad about and why she wouldn't talk to me.

I called David that night and he said, "Come on down," but then he called back a few minutes later saying I could come down after his mom left...which I knew was Linda's doing and I thought was very childish...why couldn't she even face me? I got a call back from David saying it was ok to come down now so I packed up all the emails and I took off for his house.

When I got there both David and Jessie were playing video games in his room. I said I needed to talk to them so they followed me down the hall to the master bedroom and we started talking. I told them that I didn't think their mom liked me because otherwise she would have let me come down when I had first called and she would have faced me. I brought out the emails and let them read them. They continually raised question after question, which I wanted them to do because I felt this was my extended family and so they would try to help me out...I even went as far as beginning to call David 'my little brother'.

We finished talking and Jessie said she was going to put a note on the computer for her mom asking her why. I was very apprehensive about that because somehow I knew Linda would take it the wrong way; she seemed to me to be that type of 'everybody's out to get me' person. David wanted to keep the emails for himself so he could continue reading them and I said he could.

I finished up the night by giving David the movie *Free Willy*, which I had promised to give him, and then I told them that this was the last night I would probably be seeing them because their mother would probably take everything the wrong way and I would be banned from seeing them ever again. Jessie said that her mother wouldn't do that. I said I would always love them no matter what and then I left.

Shortly after eleven p.m., when Linda got home from work that day, I found an email stating that she had found the emails in David's room and had seen what Jessie had written to her on the computer. They had all discussed the situation and decided that I could no longer see them again. In another email Linda wrote to me she said that what I'd done to her kids was like child abuse, which to this day I still don't understand.

To say that I was devastated by what had transpired was a great understatement. I was torn that I was never going to see David again and my actions that followed showed that. The last thing I emailed her for a while was asking her if I could see them one last time to say goodbye, but she said no.

I would constantly bug her at work after this, and I would also tell anyone and everyone who cared what she had done and that I felt that it was unfair. I was like a kid who had lost his favorite toy and I couldn't understand or even process it, so I took to whining about it. I am still devastated to this day about it and I wish it had never happened because I felt I'd lost the one person in this world that mattered to me most, and I had to deal with the fact that I was never going to get him back in my life.

After David was no longer in my life and I was forced to still work with his mother things were very hard for me, I couldn't stand to see her face because it would always remind me of him. Every time I saw Linda after that I got this very acidic feeling in my stomach and there was nothing I could do to make it go away, but it left after she passed by me and went in the other direction.

I would only be guessing of course, but I think that was the beginning of the end of my seven, almost eight-year career with Spears...without the P. After David was out of my life I was so depressed that I really didn't want to go to work anymore, but I knew I had to; everything for me had changed.

I'd spent all this time being a goody-two-shoes and doing what everybody told me and when they told me to do it, but now I just started doing what I wanted and when I wanted while I was at work. The calls were only supposed to take a four or five minutes on average, but on several days I probably had a thirty-minute average, that's because sometimes I would actually take a call and instead of getting right down to business I would take my time and shoot the breeze with them for over an hour.

There was one time when this supervisor actually saw that I was on the phone for an hour, but I blamed it on the customer, stating that he wouldn't get off the phone. I spent time with people on the phone that I shouldn't have and one day my team manager's manager stuck his head out of the office and told me to stop flirting. I didn't know it then, but that was strike one.

I started getting up from my seat all the time just to walk over to other people's pods just to say hi to them or shoot the breeze or conduct some sort of business with them. All the while my phone was in a kind of 'pause' mode, which is not supposed to be done. When my supervisor called me on it, which was strike two, I started pushing the envelope even more and I came to work one day wearing a shirt that said 'bite me'. I knew it was a shirt advertising a crab shack, and I knew the connotation that others would get from it, but I just didn't care. I was stopped by a supervisor and told not to wear that shirt again, which I didn't.

I noticed one of the head honchos talking to the supervisor before he came and told me not to wear that shirt again, and I asked the supervisor if the honcho had told him to say that. In true supervisor fashion he backpedaled, and he said something like, "Well some might take it as offensive."

I went DIRECTLY into that head honcho's office, told him about the situation and told him that if someone had a problem with my shirt then they needed to come and see me directly, not hinting that I knew it was him. He admitted that it was him that said that…that's about as vindictive as I can ever get.

I had written down some information about a call and I was on the phone transferring one person to somebody else, only I didn't hang up, I just muted my phone so I couldn't take another call till I got my question answered. I had called a supervisor over to answer my question when my supervisor said she wanted to speak to me...strike three, I was out. The one thing that was strange was the fact that when I was in this little room getting fired, I'd been there for almost eight years and there was no 'I'm sorry we have to let you go' or anything like that, there was just one of the head honcho's saying, "You've made a lot of sales." I was getting fired and he wasn't worried about firing me, he was just concerned about how many sales he was going to lose; I wanted to hit him.

My life with Spears, take away the P, ended and I had to find something real quick because, by this time, I kind of really loved getting a paycheck and I didn't have one anymore so I needed a way to get another one.

I went to work for this company that was basically 411, and it was ok for a little while, but I wasn't catching on like I wanted or needed to and it was frustrating me; I was angry all the time so I just told them I had family problems and I left; I've never gone back since.

My next job was working for a telemarketing company and I was activating cell phones, which was a pretty good job and I liked it very much. I ended up working there for about a month. During that one month I had a pretty fun time, not as much as the first company I worked for, but I expected that. I got to know a lot of fun people in that company and the last day I spent there they did something that I never expected them to do, nobody else had ever done it...they took me to International House Of Pancakes to say goodbye to me. I want to state here and now that I didn't get fired from that job, I'd called this other place a few months back and they had finally called me back and hired me.

My next job was for a company that I will never ever forget, and that company's name is just three letters, the beginning letters to the words 'quadruple vasectomy circumcision'...which is what I feel that company did to me. I worked for them, in total, for over a year, but it didn't take long for the stuff that they pulled to get to me. I came in one day limping because I had a boil on my leg, completely covered up so no one could see, the size of a quarter. Somebody on my team saw me limping and asked me what was wrong, and since I was the honest type and not thinking much of it, I told them that it was a boil.

I went and had the boil lanced and they said it could by MRSA, which was Methicillin-Resistant Staphylococcus aureus; that's the medical term for it. When I told this person that I had MRSA, apparently she went crazy with it because EVERYBODY knew or was talking about it within the hour. A few minutes later a supervisor came up to me and said that some people, apparently who were sitting close to me, were concerned about it and could I move; she ended up moving me WAY down to the other end of the room where was absolutely NOBODY sitting anywhere near me. That got me real pissed, but I didn't say anything to anyone about it. I did voice to the supervisor how unfair this was and that if other people had a problem with it then they should move; she agreed with me but moved me anyway.

About a half an hour after I got moved this other lady from human resources asked me to go speak with her, which I did. She said that because of what I had said and the fact that everybody was freaking out about it, she was going to send me home for the rest of the day. I only had a few more hours left to go in my shift so it didn't make much sense to me, but I went home anyway.

The thing that floored me was the fact that as I started walking down the stairs I realized I'd better go back and make sure I was getting paid vacation for this because they were the ones making me leave. However, she had the nerve to say to me, "Oh, you want to get paid," luckily for her I'm not a violent man. I had been told several times not to stop and talk to the security guard people because 'they have a job to do', but I went ahead and did it anyway because I'm just that type of friendly person. I got into trouble from the big boss many times for this because he would see me talking to them...I never understood why he didn't see the others that did the exact same thing.

There was a woman there by the name of Catherine that I'd grown to love very much while I was working there and we both hit it off like we had known each other all our lives. Every day that I came into work she would always come in an hour after me so I tried to sit where there was a place close to me where she could sit. When I saw Catherine I would say, "Hi, mommy," and she would respond with, "Hi, son."

Catherine told me that I reminded her of one of her own sons and when she went to work her other son would ask how his brother, me, was doing. We would almost always sit next to each other and I would come in wearing these shirts with funny sayings on them. She would write the sayings down on a notepad that she had so she could take them home to her son and they could laugh about them. I always got along great with everybody, but I think I got along with her because I told her about my life and she had sympathy for me, but that was clearly not the only reason we liked each other.

She was about twenty years older than me and I did love her like a son to a mother and she loved me the exact same way, and that's what made the day I got fired so hard for me.

The day that I heard she had a heart attack I was so sad because it was like I was missing my best friend. I asked for everybody to get individual cards together, then I would give them to someone who knew her address and he would either mail or take them to her. There weren't a lot of cards in the pile and that kind of made me feel bad so I took it upon myself to buy her roses and have them delivered to her home; she liked that very much, she said.

The day I got fired from that place is one of those days that will stick in my mind forever because of the way I felt I'd been treated by upper management for the boil incident and the manner in which I was fired. I had two supervisors during my one year at that place and I told BOTH of them EVERYTHING that had happened in my life because I wanted them to be prepared in case I came in with attitude; they would then hopefully understand where it was coming from.

Ever since I started working at that place I hadn't been sleeping sometimes. Although I did have nightmares that plagued me almost every night, it seemed like I had more pain and anger to deal with for some reason during this time. I would frequently stay up for a full twenty-four hours and then just crash out because I'd rather die than have to go to sleep...the nightmares were THAT bad. I've always had them bad, but for some reason during this period in my life I just could handle them less.

I hadn't slept the night before at all and I went into work. Catherine came in about an hour after me, we didn't have seats together but were soon going to remedy that situation. Catherine was sitting four seats behind me when she said there was a seat that had just opened up beside her, and I knew that's where I wanted to go. I got up and sat my backpack down at that pod and went back to my other seat because I told Catherine that I would move there at the next break. Some lady, who I found out later was one of the head honcho's, grabbed my pack from where Catherine was sitting, turned around and placed it in my hand saying, "We don't save seats here." Then I saw some other lady who was sitting just a few seats away from me a couple of minutes before sit in that VERY SAME seat that I was going to sit in after my break; that pissed me off. I have to admit that I did mumble the word 'bitch' a couple of times under my breath because that lady knew EXACTLY what she had done and why.

Catherine saw all this and a few moments later grabbed my bag from my seat and pointed to two empty seats somewhere else; I was ecstatic. I had to wait to get off the line with the customer I was talking to because THIS time I wasn't going to wait for some lady to throw my bag back in my face and say we don't save seats. I was getting frustrated because this woman I was talking to wouldn't get off the phone and I didn't want that honcho lady to come back again. One of the people on my team heard me getting upset about it and she asked me what was wrong; the next words out of my mouth got me fired.

I had finished the call with the woman and went and sat down beside Catherine, expressing my disgust at that other lady who had sat right next to her when she could obviously see that I wanted the seat. She didn't really need to move anyway because she was only one seat away from where she ended up sitting beside Catherine, who had told me that the seat was open for ME to sit in.

My supervisor called me up to his desk and asked me if I had said anything bad, and I told him, "I don't think I said anything bad." He asked me a SECOND time if I had said anything bad, and AGAIN I said, "I don't think I said anything bad."

By this time it should have been clear to me that I should have said straight out 'NO', but I was frustrated about that woman who had moved ONE seat over and sat by Catherine when she knew that Catherine wanted ME to sit there. Also I hadn't slept AT ALL the night before so at this point I was very groggy and, although I could do my job because I'd done it many times with no sleep before, I wasn't prepared for an interrogation. The fact is that I was just a total emotional mess when I was called to my supervisor's desk and I was just basically going through the motions and not understanding fully what was going on; conscious of what I was saying, but not fully aware of the ramifications. I thought he was going to ask me the same question again for a THIRD time, but he changed the question on me. My supervisor wrote 'FUCKING BITCH' down on the piece of paper and asked me if I had said it, and I said, "Yes I did."

I asked him if I was going to get fired because of it and he told me it probably wouldn't come to that. My supervisor told me to go sit down and continue doing my job, which I did, but I didn't want to because if I was going to get fired, why should I waste my time taking more calls for this company?

I talked with Catherine and told her I would probably be fired because of what he thought, with an admission from me, I had said; she was sad about it.

My supervisor told me to come with him and we went downstairs into this room with another person where I was fired on the spot. The thing that really hurt me wasn't that I was fired, because I had admitted saying what he thought I said, but the fact that he KNEW I didn't sleep at all that night before. He KNEW everything about my life and the fact that I'd been to a shrink and had been diagnosed with depression. The other fact that bugged me was the fact that he never ONCE asked me why I said what he thought I'd said.

Truth be told I was very happy to get out of there because that company had treated me like crap over the boil incident. They had treated me like crap over the fact that I was friendly and talking with security, even though other people were doing it but I was the only one singled out, and the fact that he fired me knowing what he knew. He knew how I felt about Catherine, not so much though because I really didn't advertise it to him. He knew about my depression and about my tiredness, and yet instead of doing the 'human' thing, he did the 'corporate' thing. Even though it probably doesn't matter to him, I lost a lot of respect for him that day.

He was sensitive to the fact that I didn't have a ride home, so he asked me if I wanted to go use the phone in the break room to call my parents. I wanted to kill him at that moment because if he had compassion for that, then why didn't he have compassion knowing everything he knew about me? Whether I said a bad word or not is NOT the issue, the issue is that man didn't have any fucking compassion…he was just being a corporate ass, not a human being.

There is a great song by Culture Club, one of my favorite groups. They have a song and the title happens to be something that I aspire to do with everyone and everything in life, and if he is ever reading this book or told about this book, I want to ask him one question, and that is, *If The Lord Can Forgive Why Can't You?*

I wasn't done with the company that had fired me just yet because I had something else that I was going to try courtesy of a friend named Linda, who said I should try to get in contact with the 'higher-up' at that company and explain the situation. Linda said, "Certainly your good marks and things should count for something,"...they counted for shit.

I called the 'higher-up' at the company and I spoke to his secretary, who said I could have a meeting with him on such and such a date in his office. When that date was nearing she suddenly called back and said that he had been very busy and didn't have a lot of time so it would have to be a phone conversation and it probably wouldn't last very long. Translation: 'We fired your ass already and we don't really want to have anything more to do with you so we'll give you as little a bone as possible and make sure you can't chew it.'

The higher-up did call me though and we talked for a little while, he made sure he knew that there was someone else in the room with him...in my opinion people who are just trying to cover their ass do that. I read him a long email that I had written to Linda detailing what had gone on. I thought maybe that would strike some kind of cord with him and possibly I could get my job back, but after I got done reading I could tell he wasn't even paying attention because he said, "Are you done reading?"

I tried to extol my virtues and I said that I had been exemplary when I was there just to see what he would say. He said that I hadn't been exemplary and proceeded to tell me the times he had seen me talking with security after he told me not to, he even told me about another security guard he'd seen me talking to, but he didn't get the chance to reprimand me for that.

First off, I'd like to say that when you are talking to a former employee, whether that person was fired or not, you do NOT, when someone tries to build themselves up, say 'no you weren't'. That is just a tacky and tactless thing to say. Secondly, when I told him that I didn't say what my supervisor thought I said, he told me, "That is your perception." I cannot believe a man like this is allowed to be a head honcho of a business. First he needs to learn manners, and then he needs to learn tact. I knew I wasn't getting anywhere with him being so close-minded and ignorant so I figured I'd just better end the conversation and hang up the phone right then and there because if not, I was afraid that I was going to say something that I would regret.

I don't regret being hired by that company or being friends with some of its employees because some of them were great to talk to and became great friends, I do regret, however, that I didn't say what I should have said all along. I regret saying that I didn't say what they thought I said because I was really going to miss that place. I also regret ever being friends with some of the people that work for that company because it's hard to believe that in this day and age some people are still 'corporate' minded and have NOT grasped the 'human' factor.

Now that you've read my book and you know my personal story, I think it's safe to say that I've gone through my own personal hell, I've even dragged some people along for the ride. There is a phrase that I have said throughout my life that applies to anyone and everyone, and it most certainly applies to me, many people have heard me say it: adapt or die…I'm not ready to die.

CHAPTER 8:

DEALING WITH PAIN BRAD'S WAY

Some people don't know how to deal with their pain. Some people bottle their pain up inside until they eventually implode, with disastrous circumstances. Those disastrous circumstances could be extreme like thinking everything is going wrong and the whole world would be a lot better off without them so they decide that they might as well end their life. On the other hand the reaction might be small in scale, like saying the wrong thing at the wrong time, sometimes you can just about get away with that scenario if the person to whom you said this thing knows you and knows what you've been through so they are willing to overlook it from time to time. Sometimes the small scenario can, however, lead to big losses like a job or a very good friend, and sometimes even family that doesn't understand what you have been through and are still going through.

Some people are very reactionary, they feel anger or pain and they lash out like they are being attacked. Reactionary people are very often the ones who get fired from jobs for something so small that a person that hasn't dealt with tremendous pain wouldn't get caught doing. Reactionary people sometimes hear something said about them or read something about them and react in a very negative way. They say something or do something that has unforeseen consequences which irrevocably change their lives forever, and they don't see that they did anything wrong. The reactionary person can on occasion foresee the bad thing that they are about to do or say, but they feel like another person at that instant is controlling them and they are powerless to stop it. People like that are very honest and will almost always own up to the fact that they did something wrong, and at that time try to barter to save what might become lost because of what they did or said.

I find reactionary people most often ALWAYS have to be right. When there is an argument, no matter if the other person is correct or not, the other person is in the wrong. Reactionary people must get away from this way of thinking before it totally destroys them and the people around them that love them…I mean truly love them. Those same reactionary people, if they hear the words 'I love you' or experience any kind of affection, they are drawn to it, whether it is good or bad for them.. This type of person tends not to throw the words 'I love you' around very lightly because they know what it means when other people say it and then they find out that those people really didn't mean it. It's been my understanding that if you get to know a type of person like that and they say 'I love you' to you, then you better hang on to that person as a friend or whatever that person might represent to you because you will NEVER be let down by them. They know what being let down means. Reactionary people tend to get hurt a lot. I know, because I am a reactionary type of person.

You can, however, learn not to be a reactionary person. It takes love, patience, and guidance from someone you trust VERY much. Do not, I repeat DO NOT try and get help from someone you just met or someone you know is not going to be there for very long. This will only be detrimental to you. I am not, however, saying don't talk to them or tell them certain things because you may find that telling people you know about the things that bother you or telling someone about your past helps to unburden you or help resolve issues or guilt you may feel because you think you did something wrong. In some cases it may help the listener deal with things in their past, and in some cases you may be making that other person feel useful and you may strike up a friendship that you never knew could have existed if you hadn't said a word. Just be careful about who you say things to because, as hard as it is to believe, there are people out there that are only out for themselves. There are people out there in this world that only want to hurt people and aren't satisfied unless you are hurting, so please pick and choose wisely who you tell things to. Once that person knows you and you know them VERY WELL, then, and only then, should you ask them to try and help you, by this time, hopefully, they will not only know you and WANT to help, but it will make them feel great to help YOU conquer YOUR demons and what makes you reactionary.

As I have discussed in this book, I've had a lot of things to deal with in my past and I am still dealing with those things on a day-to-day basis. You can tell yourself all you want that you've dealt with your demons and you're over them, but it's been my experience that you are never really over them. In time the pain lessens, but the memories are still there; they still linger and they still might get to you from time to time, but you have to find ways to deal with those feelings when they rear their ugly head.

I am going to tell you the way I deal with my demons in hopes that it will help you deal with yours. First of all I have to tell you that I am NOT a professional and this in NO WAY is to deter you from getting professional help if you need it, Lord knows we all need a little professional help now and then.

I found music to be my saving grace so to speak. I don't just listen to the music, I feel the music and become the lyrics. Listen to the lyrics of a song and ask yourself if what you hear can apply to you in any way, shape, or form. If the lyrics can be applied to you, then listen to the song over and over again. Start singing the lyrics to the song, and of course you'll find yourself emulating the artist at first. After you have heard the song and started singing it the way the artist would, next try adding your OWN voice to it. You're probably thinking to yourself, *What do you mean add my own voice to it, I'm already singing?* What I mean by adding your own voice to it is the inflections in your voice; let yourself FEEL the words in your mind and then sing with those same feelings. If there's no shouting in the piece of music you are singing, but you feel angry during that moment and you FEEL what the lyric is saying to you emotionally, then by all means go ahead and scream your damn head off, just be weary of next-door neighbors or people in the room next to you. Now you can move to the music. What do I mean by move to the music you ask? I don't mean moving to the beat or the vibration of the music, that I think defeats the purpose of this kind of therapy I like to do. I mean you have to move your body to the way that the lyrics make you feel. If you feel during the song that a particular lyric makes you want to raise your hands, then by all means raise your hands. Do what the music makes you feel and I can assure you after you get done singing, you will be a changed person.

The most important piece of information that I can give you that you should do is after you listen to the lyrics that get you in touch with your pain and anger, you MUST listen to a song that is very soothing to you. This should be a song that doesn't make you think, a song that you can just groove to. After doing this therapeutic exercise, I feel that you will become more aware of the things that anger you and the things that frustrate you, and you won't be powerless anymore to stop it because you will have a place in your mind where you can go. Doing this exercise will also open doors to other ways of dealing with pain, frustration and anger.

If you are in therapy, or you just need to speak to someone and have problems expressing how you feel, find a song with lyrics which can help others understand how you feel. You can record certain songs to a CD, iPod, or whatever you would like and take them down to that shrink or that friend that won't listen to you and tell them, 'Here, listen to this.' FIRST explain to them what that song means to YOU and how it relates to your situation with that person and THEN let them listen to the song, by that time they will be listening to it the way YOU hear it. If that person or that shrink you play that music for is an open-minded person, then they will be able to relate to you much better and hopefully you and that person will come to a better understanding of each other.

The next way I like to deal with anger is by playing a computer game. I don't play just any computer game mind you. The game I really like to play is PINBALL, that is my favorite all-time game. The reason it is my favorite game is that it requires almost no intelligence or any hard thinking at all, which is right up my alley. I used to play pinball a lot at the bowling alleys. I used to love to go down to the arcade and play pinball there, but it gets real expensive putting quarter after quarter in the machine; now it's up to $.50. I would recommend playing a game like that with your music blaring because, at least for me, it makes you think better and puts everything into perspective. When you are playing your music loud and playing a video game that requires no concentration, you will most likely find that after you are done playing, or you have to stop to do some chores or something like that, you feel much better than you did before and you will become more centered.

If you do this all the time though, play your music while you play a mindless game, then that will defeat the purpose of this kind of therapy. You will start to come home from work or school or whatever after a hard day and turn on your music and start playing your game. At this point you will become desensitized to the effect it had when you used to start playing only in dire circumstances and it will most definitely lose its desired result...getting you through the pain.

As well as having a therapeutic effect, playing music and a mindless game only at certain times, mostly when you are younger, can also clue your parents into the fact that something is wrong as well. Your parents will be like, "Oh, he's playing that game with his music loud again, there must be something that's bugging him, let's go have a talk with him." You will have successfully opened the lines of communication to your parents so that you can have a very meaningful discussion and perhaps avoid other horrible issues later on in life.

When you are older this can help as well because if you are married, of course your spouse will wonder what's wrong and you can talk to her about it. But even if you aren't married others will take notice...I guarantee it, if they care about you, and then you can talk to them about it and get your troubles out in the open so they don't become so troublesome any longer. A mindless game with music should only be played when you are really angry and about to bust or you are really confused and don't know what the next step in your life is going to be...that, I think, is the secret to the therapy.

Reading funny things is also a good way to deal with anger. For me, MAD magazine is the best way to relieve anger inside of me. I could have the worst day I've ever had in my whole entire life, and I could also have feelings stirring around inside me of past things that I'm ashamed of or angry about, but when I come home at the end of the day or, if permitted, I can pull out that magazine right then and there and start reading, then I INSTANTLY forget about what I was ever angry about and I become transfixed by this magazine. The things that they say in MAD magazine and the situations that come out of that magazine are so funny that often times I will just burst out laughing when I'm reading and people will look at me as if to say 'What is that man doing? He's crazy being all alone and laughing like that," and then when they looked over they would see me reading my magazine and say, "Oh he's reading MAD again." Some people even have asked if they could read it after me...MAD magazine is good therapy.

Writing is also a good source of therapy for getting out anger and frustration. I wasn't always a big believer in writing down your feelings on a piece of paper because I was always the one that would say, "Why do I want to write it down? It won't help anyway." I can say with absolute certainty now that writing down your feelings really does help. I knew from listening to music that I felt certain ways about certain things, it was just that I wasn't able to verbalize the thoughts that I had so I looked to the singers I was listening to who could verbalize my feelings for me. The thing I needed to realize was that I never had to verbalize those feelings...I could write them down.

Verbalizing something and writing it down are two totally

different things. Today, if you asked me how I felt after what has happened to me, I would probably be able to tell you, but I would just be stuttering over my words. I may give you a couple of sentences that are difficult for you to understand because you weren't in the same situation as I was. However, if you asked me to write it down, then I could probably take some time to think about what I wanted to say and also be able put it in terms that a person who hasn't gone through it could understand.

Writing is a great tool. When I say writing is a great tool, I'm not talking about waiting until you are on your computer to compose your thoughts, because by the time you get to your computer maybe that thought will have gone out of your mind and you wish you could get it back, but you can't...I've done that. Writing is actually taking a pen or pencil to paper and jotting down your thoughts right then and there, you can clean it up later on the computer if your writing looks like a doctor wrote it. Writing can happen any time night or day.

The other night I was lying in bed trying to fall asleep and couldn't, we've all been there, when this lyric came into my head and I thought to myself, *Gee, that's good, I need to get it down on paper right away.* So I flipped on the light at three a.m., wrote it down and I was able to get back to sleep.

There are other times when I think of something that early in the morning, but I'm too lazy to get up to write it down and the next morning I'm be mad at myself because it was a good line and now I can't remember it. Writing is good, it's therapeutic, and in some ways it can help save your life.

I've talked about how I deal with pain, but now I want to talk a bit about the ramifications of people that have been through types of situations like this.

Grooming seems to be a less important factor to someone who has been repeatedly sexually assaulted than it is for someone who hasn't had to go through that kind of an ordeal. Let's take physical appearance for an example. As a person who has been through this type of ordeal grows up, they have this feeling of not caring what they look like, so they may go out looking scruffy or unshaved or with tasseled hair or things like that because to them people are looking at them for one thing and one thing only. Then, however, there are other people that place a great deal of importance on what they look like and constantly want to recreate the look they had when they were younger because that's when they received what they perceived at that time to be love.

The important thing is to recognize when you are in that mindset and change your way of thinking. You may not always recognize when you are in fact in that mindset, it's not as if a switch suddenly goes off and changes you into a different person all of a sudden...like perhaps if you were a psycho, so let me give you some advice. There are several different ways of identifying when you are in that mindset. A good way is to ask a close friend to basically monitor your behavior. I'm not saying that person has to camp out at your front door or hook you up to strange devices or anything like that. The friend, after spending time with you and getting to know you very well, would be able to recognize when you are slipping into that bad habit. Let's get that right out in the open right away. It is a bad habit because it may not only be physically detrimental; it can be psychologically detrimental as well. Your friend may be able to snap you out of this habit.

The person you trust to do this for you must be a very good friend so that number one they won't witness this from you and then running to tell somebody else, 'Hey, do you know what so and so just did?" And two, that person won't be freaked out by you when you suddenly go into that mindset and will understand and will help you through it.

They have to know how to snap you out of it delicately though or otherwise you may grow to resent that person and probably not trust them anymore at all; and trust is a VERY IMPORTANT issue for anyone, but more so to someone dealing with these issues. The two of you need to come up with some kind of trigger word or little action that only you understand (because it's nobody else's business) that will let you know that this behavior is happening. It's ultimately up to the person displaying the behavior to change it, but friends can help identify when it's happening so the behavior can lessen and then hopefully disappear forever. I say hopefully because in some people the behavior never completely goes away; it's always lurking somewhere in the background ready and waiting to rear its ugly head.

Hygiene also seems to be a less important factor to someone dealing with these particular kinds of issues. Bathing seems to be a particularly troublesome issue for some. A person going through these types of issues takes to bathing in an extreme way, both positively and negatively; let me explain what I mean.

There are some people that will bathe constantly to get those bad feelings and bad touches off of them, even though they can't because the psychological damage has already been done. There are also some people that will not bathe for several days because inside their minds they feel very dirty anyway, and may also have been told that they were, so in turn, the outside of their body gets to looking a lot like how the inside of their mind feels, very dirty...it's all psychological. This person may also like the way that he smells when he hasn't bathed for a while because, and normal society wouldn't know this but, when he was younger the acts that he was doing caused him to sweat a great deal. It is possible that he has been around a lot of sweaty men so sweat doesn't bother him, and the intoxication of his sweat takes him back to where he was when he was younger, and that's a safe thing for him because he doesn't know how to be any other way.

When a person feels very dirty inside and they look and smell a little dirty on the outside, then they are often shunned and made to feel worse because of it. It's important for us to lift up people that feel like that. We must reach deep down past our discomfort about that situation and help them because they may need it, and you never know how many lives you may change just by showing that you care. We must learn to break down all those psychological barriers that make us feel the way we do and treat the underlying problems.

Psychiatrists, some anyway, feel that they can treat your problems by talking about what happened as well as giving you medication because, as they are fond of saying, there may be a chemical imbalance in your brain. I don't buy that chemical imbalance crap. I feel if those psychiatrists when through the things that I went through, then they would be acting a little differently too. I try not to listen to them if I can help of it because for all their knowledge and experience, coupled with whatever you decide to tell them when you're lying on that couch for an hour, they still don't know the REAL you...and they never will. And let's face I, we don't tell them the WHOLE truth, do we?.

When someone has been violated repeatedly in a sexual manner, most often times they will mistake that for love and keep making the same mistake again and again and never really find the love that they are actually looking and longing for. Love is in many forms, but love is NOT sexual contact between a child and an adult…even if you are a child and you said 'uh ok', you are too young to really know any better, but that adult should DEFINITELY know better.

When a child grows up in the kind of an environment where sexual contact is commonplace, love can be a very confusing thing for that child to comprehend. When growing up, and also when grown, that person who experienced negative sexual contact will take any form of affection thrown their way, leaving them in a very vulnerable state of mind. If anyone just says 'hi' to a person in that state of mind then that person will want to gravitate to the one that told them 'hi'. That person will tend to want to be a part of that other person's life and want to be around them all the time. This may come across as a little annoying, and the person may feel like their space is being totally invaded. But to the vulnerable person, the other person said 'hi' so in their mind they are totally being accepted into the other person's whole life because to people with this kind of problem the word 'hi' is just like saying 'I love you'.

When a person has grown up with inappropriate sexual activity all their lives, they tend to 'own it'. What do I mean when I say 'own it'? When I say this I mean that person tends to become what he emulated when he was younger or tends to exhibit signs of that behavior. What are the types of behavior you need to look for when identifying the type of person or personality I am describing? The type of person I am describing usually tends to keep his sexual preference a secret, most often because he doesn't know what type he prefers. He will most often go with the flow if he's in a conversation with a crowd who are talking about doing something to this girl or banging that girl just so he won't be labeled, but all the while he is looking across the room thinking that the guy sitting at the opposite table is very cute. This is NOT to be confused with the atypical gay guy who doesn't want their friends to know that he is gay because then he will get harassed, or even worse.

When a person is young and is around young boys who are using them sexually and guys who are as well, when they get older they tend to 'hang on' to the feelings they had back then. The young boys who have now grown up and have been around sex with boys and men all their lives tend to think in very sexual ways and have very sexual thoughts about men and boys. Both when it is not appropriate, and especially at times when they don't want that feeling to make itself known, even if it's only known to them. That sexually charged, not his fault at all, man may be surfing on the Internet totally innocently and come across a picture of a man in a Speedo, while he's searching for men's underwear, and get totally aroused...that is an example of not wanting to have that feeling known.

At other times he may be actively looking for it because some part of his brain misses it from his younger days and he comes across a website where there are pictures of shirtless boys. He can sit there in the privacy of his own home and gratify himself to those pictures and for that particular moment it's ok...it's normal to him. This man could be in a store just shopping around and see a young boy playing a game or running around or something like that, he will actually stop and stare at that boy and think sexual thoughts automatically, most times they just come without thought and can't be stopped. Other times that same man will go to a place like Sea World, where there are literally hundreds of shirtless boys in Speedos around, and he will just enjoy the view like a normal person would enjoy the night sky. The man will not actively admit to anyone that he does this because, even though in his mind it's perfectly fine because that's all that he knows, all the rest of society is a different beast all together.

Society tells us it's wrong to have these feelings and it's wrong to act on these feelings, but yet when someone has these thoughts or feelings they cannot go to society and tell them that they have this problem. They have to go to a psychiatrist in some little office hidden out of society's way to go and talk about their problem and hopefully get it solved. Most times the person with those sexual thoughts will not want to get his situation solved at all because for the longest time that's all that he has known and all that he has felt, and if he goes to a psychiatrist and gets his problem solved, will he still be the same man? Will he like the man that he will become? I have a bit of news for you all; your situation cannot be solved. The ramifications of your situation can be lessened, however. The way that you can lessen the ramifications of this is most definitely by talking to someone about your problem.

Guys in this situation are the ones that keep things bottled up and don't let any personal feelings out. Oh sure, that person will say some things like 'when I was younger I was molested', or something like that, but they won't expand on it at all. When I say that a person will say something like they were molested I am talking about the older person that may or may not understand the ramifications of what happened to them, but they realize it happened and they realize there is no going back and undoing it.

When sexual situations JUST HAPPENED, you don't want to deal with it at all. When this sort of thing happens you tend to think that you are dirty or that you are no good, or worse yet only good for one thing…a good time. If it's a one-time incident and it never happens again, sure it stays with you, but it probably doesn't have the same kind of impact as it does to those who have it repeatedly done to them.

When you have a person or persons repeatedly treating you as a revolving sex machine, or toy if you will, you tend to become numb to it. What I mean is that you tend to expect it happening all the time so you learn to shut off the part of your body and your brain that feels anything. I'm not talking about being a hooker as in you can shut off your emotions and just do what you are there to get paid to do, even though that has emotional consequences all of its own. What I'm talking about is that you can shut yourself off, for that time, from any emotional and/or physical pain. Hey, wait a minute, aren't I describing what a hooker does? In part, yes, that's what a hooker is and does, but a hooker makes that conscious choice to do what she is doing and also to be paid the amount that she is being paid…although her pimp might say differently, whereas someone who is being repeatedly sexually used doesn't have that choice in any way, shape, or form.

EPILOGUE

First and foremost I am NOT trying to absolve myself of any crimes I have committed in my life. I am NOT trying to give excuses for my bad behavior by saying my behavior was a direct result of how I was treated. I do believe, however, that had I not endured what I have gone through in my lifetime, the crimes that I have committed would not have happened.

You will notice that throughout this book it's been somewhat, I hope you feel that way, humorous. You will also notice that there have been some sad points. I don't think of them as sad points though because those times in my life helped to make me the person I am today.

There is a line in a song by a child named Declan Galbraith that says something about rain falling and flowers growing, I will paraphrase because I don't feel like being sued for using someone else's words. I really believe in the message that in everyone's life a little rain must fall, because without the rain we can't grow into the people we need to become. I DON"T believe in an 'eye for an eye' mentality. That is the MAIN reason I wrote this book, so people could find another outlet for their anger instead of taking it out on the innocent and the helpless.

Let's stop all the fussing and fighting and name-calling and pointing of fingers and learn to get along. Let's stop all this he said, she said, business and learn to live in peace and harmony with one another, we can do it if we try. When that person who is sitting next to you on the bus, if you don't have a car, has his head down or whimpering about something, ask him if he's all right. When your coworker, whom you don't even know because when you go to work you're just there to do a job and then get home, looks like they have something on their minds, go ahead and ask them what it is. If they don't want to tell you, they will let you know...sometimes they feel better though knowing someone stopped long enough to care.

Go into work tomorrow and just go by everybody's desk and say "Hi, how are you today?" and then don't just walk away, stand there and listen to their response...it might just change your life.

People say all the time 'forgive and forget', 'live and let live', 'whatever will be will be'...I don't believe in those sayings. First of all if you have been through a very traumatic experience, your brain won't let you forget. You can lessen the impact over time, but you can never forget what was done to you...the ironic point about that is the person or persons that did this horrible thing might just soon forget about it as quickly as it happened. If you happen to have been victimized and then you yourself turn around and victimize someone in that very same way, then it is much more difficult to forget because you have this bad thing that happened to you going around in your head, and NOW you also have the bad thing that you did to someone else going around in your head. If you don't know how to deal with it quickly, it can really mess you up.

The second quote 'live and let live' is to me the most horrific thing that you can do. If something bad happens to you, you don't just want to live with it, you have to let it out and let others know that this kind of stuff still goes on in the new millennium. Once you do that and get your voice heard, it will not only help cleanse you, it may just help that other person that you told deal with what's been going on in their life...when you tell someone something, you just have NO IDEA how many lives you touch.

The third quote 'whatever will be will be' is just wrong. YOU yourself make your life what it is. Yes, there are unforeseen circumstances that may happen to you which at the time you can't prevent, but you are the only one that can ultimately deal with them and choose the way you live with the pain. Yes, I said pain...I said pain because if something like what happened to me happened or is happening to you, it is VERY painful to deal with and the scars that are left are permanent. There is no way to get rid of the scars, but there are different ways of dealing with them, and I hope that you, by having read this book, choose to deal with them the right way.

Let me now give you a top-ten list of songs that have helped me get through and deal with things, and also the reason why those songs mean what they do to me. After all, songs mean different things to different people, but how are others supposed to know what they mean to us, the people that have been victimized and have in turn victimized others, if we don't tell them? For instance, a child can be up in his room listening to heavy metal and his parents don't understand why he even likes that type of music, but do the parents ever go into his room, listen to the lyrics and ask why? ...NO.

1. *Will You Be There* by Michael Jackson. This song means so much to me because it was the song I listened to just before I tried to commit suicide, and now it's the song of my salvation. Its message is just basically, after all the pain and sorrow and hurt that I'm going through, will you be there for me?

2. *Thriller* by Michael Jackson. This song reminds me of my brother from start to finish. From the door creaking open in the

beginning until the laughter at the end the song helped me understand what my brother was, in relation to me, and the song still helps me to this very day put things into their proper perspective when I have mixed feelings about him.

3. *Private Dancer* by Tina Turner. This song makes me think of what I have turned into as a result of what I've been through.

4. *Heal The World* by Michael Jackson. I went out and bought the song *Will You Be There* on the Dangerous album and this song was on it, and when I heard it I FINALLY stopped thinking the world was about me and MY pain...we all have a whole world to protect.

5. *Dangerous* by Michael Jackson. When I hear it, I think of the first night my brother touched me and the aftermath of it.

6. *Making Love Out Of Nothing At All* by Air Supply. From an early age I was told that I WAS nothing, and I can't believe there are actually lots of people who look at a nothing like me and see love.

7. *Is It Scary* by Michael Jackson. How I truly see myself. Some people expect me to be one way while others expect me to be another and I try to please them all, somewhere along the line I lost who **I** really am.

8. *Victims* by Culture Club. I can't help but feel I've been one of these all my life.

9. *Do You Remember* by Phil Collin from 'Serious Hits Live'. This one is about my mom for me because she's had so many problems ever since I told her 'just a little', and things have never been like they were.

10. *What's Love Got To Do With It* By Tina Turner. The reason I'm hesitant about ever working with children again, people will always be asking that question.

There you have it, at least ten of my favorite songs and how they've helped me deal with things…I hope they help you as well.

www.ingramcontent.com/pod-product-compliance
Lightning Source LLC
Chambersburg PA
CBHW030013290326
41934CB00005B/328